This book is dedicated to my children Semisi, Pinomi and Aristotle who seldom hear me talk about God.

LIVE A LIFE OF MIRACLES

...with God...

SEMISI PULE

Copyright © Rainbow Enterprises Books

Publisher: Rainbow Enterprises Books

ISBN: 978-1-98-851189-4

All rights reserved. No part of this book shall be reproduced, in any way, without prior written permission from the writer and copyright holder.

NOTE:

Most of the information for this book were the author's own experience and knowledge gained over a period of 50 years as a Christian. Additional evidence are added from Wikipedia, Google and the Bible. The King James Version, New International Version and Online Bible Sources were used. It is impossible to list all sources but suffice it to say, that as Christians believe, all the information came from God. The revelations I use to explain the trinity for example would be totally new to all and like St Paul I believe it to be God's revelations.

This story is about my early years in the Kingdom of Tonga, which is a small island nation in the South West Pacific about 2,379 kilometers from New Zealand and 5,212 kilometers from Australia. Tonga is next door neighbors with Samoa and Fiji in the Pacific Ocean.

Additional information about Jesus Christ and Christianity is added to support what I believe is God's actions on earth.

INTRODUCTION

You may not believe it's possible, to live a life with God's miracles, but being alive and experiencing the world through the senses is in itself a miracle of creation. We tend to take everything for granted but as soon as we realize that we are part of something bigger and more amazingly wonderful our spiritual journey will begin.

I would like to write this book about the miracles of a life with God. Most people will have their own appreciation and realization of God's role in their lives. I want to share my own experiences as a child of God. God has led me to arrive at this point in life understanding how he had shaped my life.

I used to go to church every week as a child. Now I go maybe once a month, but as you can tell, I do study the Bible and Christian history and try to understand them in my own life experience.

In every major development and event, I can see God's hand in it. There is no other explanation.

Sometimes God will destroy my dreams and efforts because it will lead to a less successful existence.

In addition, I think God led me to a 'higher understanding' of what eternal damnation mean. It is a very important issue in Christian philosophy because the ultimate aim of the Christian faith is becoming one with Christ. Becoming one with the Holy Trinity. Becoming one with eternity. Becoming one with God.

Eternal damnation is to be avoided at all cost, in a Christian's journey to find God and his eternal blessing. Eternal damnation will prevent one from becoming one with God and live the eternal existence promised in Jesus Christ, his death and resurrection. Pope Francis did say in one of his sermons that souls who do not return to God are simply lost or destroyed. This is probably what is meant by 'eternal death' in Christianity.

I really wonder what it means, but it is possible that souls cannot exist by themselves. They either return to God or be born again as proposed by reincarnation supporters. If they linger by themselves on earth or anywhere else, they simply disappear or is swallowed up by something bigger than themselves. We need to study OBE (out of body experiences) and NDE (near death experiences) to understand the soul a bit more. A figure of 20 million people in the USA alone, experienced OBE or NDE sometime in their lives.

We shall see later in the last part the evidence accumulated by Science to prove that souls do exist.

You will note that I use my science training to try and explain God using empirical evidence. This is important in our human understanding of the infinite and why God is such a powerful entity. At the same time God is so very human as part of every living thing on earth, as part of man. As man himself. This is probably why the Christian Bible points out that man was made in God's Image. Man is God with a finite existence on earth but an infinite existence as God. That is key to everything in religion. Because we are part of God, it is our destiny to return to God when our earthly existence ends. As we shall see later it is not a simple matter, returning to God is a journey itself that one must make as a pilgrim in life.

This book is about my own experience and why I think it was God's intervention in my life. I explain how God has shaped my life in the hope that others can also see how God help them in theirs. Many people complain about the problems they have and the destruction that happens to them and their properties. But if they look a bit closer and think about it, maybe God is closing that door because he wants to open a better one for them. We should understand that this life on Earth is not the real one, from a spiritual point of view. Our real existence begin after the earthly body dies as we shall see later in the stories of OBE and NDE individuals.

In my book, The Anti-Christ, I try to point out that there is also another powerful entity on earth. The one the apostle John referred to as 'out there' as opposed to the one 'inside us'. John is talking about God inside us and the Anti-Christ is the 'one out there' or also known as Satan, the Devil, the Evil One. I describe him as the 'polar opposite of God'. He is the cause of our 'eternal damnation' because if he wins then we cannot be with God, which is a topic that need further investigation.

Sometimes events occur in our lives which are caused by the 'polar opposite of God' or the one we call the Devil, the Anti-Christ. That is the best argument for keeping God on our side because only God is stronger than 'the one out there', who seek to destroy us. God will help us survive our earthly existence and return to his infinite warmth and power. Most of the recorded ODEs and NDEs speak of a very vivid and real world, much more beautiful than our earth, which they have visited after they die, but they are told, usually by dead relatives and friends, to return to earth because their purpose in life has not been fulfilled.

Millions of people have had an OBE or NDE and all their accounts are similar, they can't be all wrong!

CONTENT

Part I. The Early Years

Chapter 1. A Place to Worship..........................2
Chapter 2. Blessing from a man of God 22
Chapter 3. A greater path is opened for me......33
Chapter 4. Always first in Class.....................43
Chapter 5. Encounters with a parallel universe..48

Part II. The Holy Trinity

Chapter 1. The Trinity........................70
Chapter 2. What is Hell?..........................84
Chapter 3. The Ark of the Covenant...........88

Part III. How can you tell God's influence in your life?

Chapter 1. God's hand or random event?.....95
Chapter 2. Is your life full of riches but still feel empty?..111

Part IV. The 5 Pillars of Christ

Chapter 1. Faith..........................122
Chapter 2. Hope..........................150
Chapter 3. Love..........................163
Chapter 4. Charity......................182
Chapter 5. Spiritual Salvation................194

Part V. The Truth about the Bible and Jesus Christ

Chapter 1. Titus Flavius 200

Part VI. Reincarnation

Chapter 1. What the Bible say 209
Chapter 2. Hinduism and Buddhism 215
Chapter 3. Scientific Evidence about the existence of the soul..........................220

PART I.

The Early Years, the Gift of the Evangelist

Chapter 1.

A place to worship

What do you think constitutes a miracle?

Merriam Webster defines a miracle as;

 'an extraordinary event manifesting divine intervention in human affairs'

In Dictionary.com it is defined as;

 'an effect or extraordinary event in the physical world that surpasses all known human or natural powers and is ascribed to a supernatural cause'.

It does mean that miracles can only be attributed to things or events that we can see immediately. It may not include changes in our lives and circumstances that we do not see or become aware of. Subtle changes that only become apparent later in life but are not immediately obvious to us in our younger days. But most times that is how changes occur in our own lives. Some events may take years to become noticeable. It is with that in mind that I relate this story of my childhood.

Primary School and Church Beginnings

As a child in Primary School, I had a friend who lives about a 10 minute walk from our house. He always invites me to come to his house and play, then we decided to go to church. That Sunday, I put on my best Sunday church clothes and we walk up to the Centenary Wesleyan Church near the Royal Palace in Nuku'alofa, Tonga. It was the biggest building and church in the country, so attending church service there was something real special.

All the kids were normally asked to use the mezzanine floor at the back of the building. There were a number of kids that usually come with their parents to church. They were the rich and elite of Nuku'alofa who attend the biggest church in the biggest building in the biggest city in the country. We all know now that Nuku'alofa is not even a city but the locals are proud of living in the capital. The service was on a loudspeaker so we can hear what the preacher was saying at the back, on the mezzanine floor.

In the Free Wesleyan Sunday church services in Tonga, there is a children's story during the service. The preacher will normally come down from the pulpit and tell the kids, who normally sit on the floor at the front, a story, and it was that part of the service I enjoyed the most. The stories will have a powerful moral message which the church hope to instill in its young generations.

After about a year of attending the Centenary FWC Service, and sometimes attending the church service at another FWC parish at a nearby suburb called Longolongo, somebody decided to build a church building next door!

It was a little congregation, known as Ha'atavake who meet at a house near the old Vaiola hospital, about 5 minutes walk away, but the hospital has moved and so it was shifted to the property next door. The congregation was usually made up of caregivers who bring their sick relatives to the hospital and needed somewhere to pray. It was tradition for the

FWC members, the biggest church group in Tonga, to attend church service every Sunday.

The Vaiola Hospital moved to Tofoa, which is a village outside Nuku'alofa. I heard from other church members that the King, His Majesty Taufa'ahau Tupou IV, wanted more land for a bigger and more modern hospital.

Because there were no hospital patrons to fill the Ha'atavake fellowship, somebody decided to move the church next door. The house they used was a residential house belonging to a family. With the hospital gone, there was no need for the church at the site and the family were happy to have their house back. I think that was why they moved. Somebody consciously made the decision, and everyone agreed, including the neighbours to move the church next door.

Why they moved next door is a miracle, it gave me a place to worship without walking 30-40 minutes. It occurred to me that out of a place where the sick were cared for came spiritual salvation for my family.

That really solved a big problem for me, because I was beginning to realize that walking to church every Sunday was also taking me to a lot of other places, as a kid. My friend and I enjoyed walking to the beach, exploring old buildings and generally spending a lot of time away from home, after church. Going to church was just an excuse to wander around the beach and generally explore all the wild places around town. God decided to close that door and open a new one for me. He gave me a place to worship and spend my time.

It did also mean, I will spend less time with my friend. The church moving next door changed my life forever. It is for that reason why I think that it was God's hand that made it happen. It was the beginning of my Christian training.

God saved my family

Not only me, but my whole family! My Dad, whom I have never seen attending a church started coming to church and also my Mum and siblings. My Dad was a heavy drinker and smoker. Every weekend, my Dad and his friends will sit around our living room and drink a carton, or a few cartons, of Steinlager. It was the most popular beer of his generation, large 750 ml bottles of Steinlager beer in a cardboard carton from New Zealand. Dad was a Senior Civil Servant and was regarded, and respected, very highly in our neighborhood and his village. He was one of the success stories from his village of Tatakamotonga. Being a Civil Servant was the pinnacle of any Tongans career during those days, before university education and university degrees from overseas became fashionable.

Although I have never seen Dad become violent after drinking he did belt me a few times for minor and even unexplained reasons. Not when he is drunk, but when he is sober.

I often wonder why Dad always belt me for minor things like playing with the neighbor's kids with no permission from him or Mum, until I visited his Mum, my grandmother in the village. She belted me with a stick for going swimming without permission. The beach was just 30 seconds walk from her house so I spent most days there. I realized that belting the kids was the normal punishment in Dad's family. Hitting the kids with a belt or stick as a disciplinary measure, what they call 'capital punishment' in New Zealand. It was the accepted method in the ancient history of Tonga, smacking the disobedient with a club on the head. Punishment was usually very severe for minor offenses.

My Mum never belt me, she would just grab a piece of skin on my stomach or hand and twist it. It hurt like hell! That was her kind of punishment. It was the only time I see her get upset, when I tease my sister, who was the youngest in the family. In the Tongan culture, the sister is the 'chiefly person', in the family and every brother must respect her and honor her. Us young boys did not know anything about that part of our culture until Mum gets upset with us. Me and the younger brothers always gets punished for teasing our sister. We found out, it is taboo for us boys to open our mouths against our sister, even in jest.

When my family started going to church, I noticed my Dad does not belt me anymore. My Mum too, she did not punish me anymore. I felt that God had done another miracle for me and my family. I no longer get belted! My Dad stopped drinking alcohol and smoking cigarettes and became a lay preacher, also becoming the Church Steward of our church, organizing the members and meeting regularly with the regional

Church Reverend thus becoming very involved in the Free Wesleyan Church administration, of our district, for many years.

My Mum became a Church Counsellor or *akonaki* in the Tongan language. I think it meant that she is now able to advise and instruct non church members on the ways of the church, probably an evangelistic rank which recruit new church members in the old days.

When I finished High School and left to study in New Zealand, in 1980, my parents were still serving as Stewards for our church which has changed location and name. It moved to another property, about 5 minutes walk, where it got a permanent site and its name changed from Ha'atavake to Kapeta. The family had donated their land for the church site. That in itself was a miracle, because the kids all moved overseas and so the church got a new administrative, evangelical and service site. There are a few stories to this family move but I cannot tell them without permission from their family members. Suffice it to say, their sacrifice had given them and others much blessing in the physical world.

My parents were also responsible for the Youth Group, who meet at our house every Friday for prayers and supportive sermons to help with their lives as young adults. A famous evangelist or church spiritual advisor will always be invited to join them and speak to the youth during those meetings. I would always sit in my room and listen to the service in the adjacent living room. I remember really enjoying it and looking forward to the Friday meetings especially the tea and cakes after.

The youth group were always at our house doing the cooking when we have the annual church fundraiser. There were several groups in the church, the youth being a separate one, which collects donations for the church. Some of the money raised goes to the main body of the church to help with costs and some is 'earmarked' for church projects like renovating the church building which was just made of particle board.

I heard a story that this particular fund raising method, called a *misinale* in the local language, began with the Rev Shirley Baker, a British Missionary, who was the first Prime Minister of Tonga after helping King George Tupou I establish the Kingdom of Tonga in

1875 with a Constitution after the Westminster Model of the United Kingdom.

Our house was always full of laughter and chatter, many times a year, as the young men and women prepare food for special occasions in church, including the *misinale*, Easter, Christmas and New Year. There's pigs to be roasted on the spit, *'umu* or earth oven to cook taro, yam, kumara, octopus in coconut cream, fish wrapped in coconut leaf, beef and lamb in coconut cream and onions wrapped in taro leaves with a banana cover, butchered pork and even salted beef from New Zealand. The young women prepare raw fish, corned beef, sweets and delicacies in the house kitchen. Cakes were baked and even doughnuts Tongan style.

Us kids we are always sitting on logs, bins, empty buckets or whatever is available and watching the men and learn how the *'umu* is done. There were no chairs. We help by doing the running around fetching anything the men need for doing the *'umu* or buy some ingredient the women forgot to buy for their recipes. My older brothers, who were in their late teens were considered to be 'young adults'. I fetch the spade for them, the bush knife, banana leaf, coconut leaf, sacks for covering the *'umu* or whatever is needed. The *'umu* has to be covered with earth as quickly as possible to keep the heat in or the food won't cook, so the men cannot run around looking for anything they need. Us kids do that while the men pile on the banana leaves, sacks and earth on top of the *'umu*.

A Tongan feast is something to behold when it is all done. Two or three meter of, banana leaf covered, woven coconut frond laid fully stacked with staple foods, sweets, delicacies of all kinds. The best foods from local and overseas markets presented for the guests to eat. Two or three suckling pigs roasted over an open fire lay steaming hot in the middle of the *pola,* the local name for the woven coconut frond which also include the food on it.

It was the best way of learning, is by doing. The deeper meaning of it, in the Christian sense, is the 'art of giving'. Our little church usually raise $4,000 or more in the annual *misinale*. In the 1970s, that was a lot of money for a small group of families, mostly young men and women, to give.

The church members, like all FWC members in Tonga like to 'sacrifice' personal wants in favor of giving to the church. Money, food and time are generously donated in the name of the Lord, Jesus Christ. It wasn't lost on us kids, the meaning of it all. For the young men and women, a training of a lifetime.

The Tongan *misinale* is legendary in the Pacific Islands where, in Rev Shirley Baker's time, they were able to raise £ 60,000 a year. It was so much money they even donated some of it to help the Methodist missions in Australia and New Zealand according to some stories.

My family history

Both my parent's ancestors were strong supporters of the Methodist Mission. Since the arrival of the first Methodists, Rev and Mrs Walter Lawry, in 1822 the Tongan mission grew and grew with the baptism of the Tu'i Ha'apai, Taufa'ahau in 1831.

My mother's great grandfather Rev Sioeli Nau became a missionary for the Methodist Mission in 1856, when the famous Tongan missionary Rev Sioeli Pulu asked George Tupou I for more missionaries and teachers.

Rev Sioeli Nau worked with Rev Sioeli Pulu on the island of Bau where his wife died in 1861. Rev Sioeli Nau moved to Kadavu where he married Akosita, eldest daughter of the Tui Kadavu. They had 10 children, 7 of which worked in the church with 3 of them as missionaries.

The story of Rev Semisi Nau's mission at Ontong Java

Rev Sioeli Nau's second son Rev Semisi Nau was selected as a missionary to Ontong Java, the largest atoll in the world, in the Solomon Islands from 1905 - 1919.

This is a story I heard as a child from family members, most probably my grandmother 'Oliva Nau, daughter of Rev Tevita Kata Nau II. Rev Tevita Kata Nau II is Rev Semisi Nau's older brother and the eldest of Rev Sioeli Nau and 'Akosita's children.

When Semisi Nau and his group arrived at the island (Ontong Java), the village Chiefs did not want them to come ashore and they stayed on the boat in the lagoon. For several months, they sang and prayed on the boat and every evening the people from shore heard the hymns and began to gather on the beach to listen, even the Chiefs began coming to listen to the singing. They ran out of food, on the boat, and one night a noise was heard as a native swimmer arrives with fresh coconuts from shore. He came every night with coconuts and food. Then one day they were told the chief had agreed for them to come ashore. They thought that it was their singing that really inspired the locals because it sounded so beautiful and melodious coming from the boat every evening.

I have read the accounts of the story of Rev Semisi Nau in many online sources, including the Solomon Is Historical Encyclopedia 1893-1978, but there is no reference to any of the singing and praying on the boat nor the swimmer and food or coconuts. It's probably just a family legend. That is why I mention it here because it is part of the family history.

They did stay on the boat for 3 months before going ashore according to the Solomon Island encyclopedia. It was a local chief in one village. Here's the except from the encyclopedia;

'For the first three months they were forced to live in a whaleboat in the lagoon because of the opposition of Chief Keapea of Luangiua and his

people. Eventually they were allowed to land at the northern village of Pelau, and were able to visit Luangiua. One year later, three churches had been built.'

The story of Rev Semisi Pule

Semisi Pule was born in 1860 to Paula Visi Masaga of Falehau, Niuatoputapu and Meleane Tokemoana of Lifuka, Ha'apai. He went to Tonga College and after successful completion of his studies he became a cadet civil servant. He worked in the Ha'apai Group as a clerk and probably as a teacher, and also in the church. In 1915, he was ordained a minister and joined the Methodist Mission. In 1824 when the Free Wesleyan Church was established he continued with the FWC until 1931. He became a retired 'Minister of the Church' in 1931 and died in 1933 in Lifuka, Ha'apai.

Rev Semisi Pule was married to Salote Mafi'ahau they had 7 children. They were working as Minister for Tatakamotonga District where his fourth son Viliami Ponepate met Pinomi Lai'atea and married her in 1928. My father Samisoni was born in March, 1929.

The church in the family

I have related the story of Rev Semisi Nau and Rev Semisi Pule just to illustrate the involvement of the Methodist Mission and Free Wesleyans in our ancestry and family. There were actually many other missionaries and church workers from our family which can be found in the story of Rev Sioeli Nau in Wikipedia.

I believe our family is blessed in many ways because of our historical involvement with missionary work and spreading the gospel in the Pacific. It came as a surprise to me that Rev Filipe Nau, father of Rev Sioeli Nau, was also a missionary in Samoa where they established Methodism as the 'Lotu Toga' (the church from Tonga).

I relate these historical ties to the church because Tongans believe that it is a blessing to give one's life to Jesus. As God says to Moses in Exodus 20:6,

'showing loving devotion to a thousand generations of those who love me and keep my commandments'

When I was a student at Auckland University, it always amazes me how much money our Methodist church members have. They always give money everyday, including Sundays, to various groups from Tonga who came to fundraise in New Zealand for various projects like schools, church buildings and so on. The weekly wage for most of the church members would be about $150 - $200 and their rent, food and other bills come out of that including donating to the church groups almost every day!

I look at those Tongan people today, some 30-40 years later, most of them have paid off their mortgage. It was only $20,000-$40,000 during the late 1970s to 1980s, but are now worth close to a million dollars. Some properties are even worth 2 million dollars! They are still doing the same giving to church projects in New Zealand and in Tonga yet they manage to pay off a mortgage! And their children too have free hold properties.

As a student, I stayed with my uncle who was the Chief Minister of the Tongan Methodist church. He travels all over New Zealand to establish new Tongan congregations. He spend most of his days in church activities. He has passed away now but all his children and his brother's children own property. Most of them free hold. I am very good at mathematics but I would not be able to give everybody a free hold property on the kind of income they were getting, yet it happened. It is just a miracle.

That is what I think God means when he said to Moses *'he will love and bless those who love him to a thousand generations'*.

It seemed that those people who gave the most money to the church are the people who are very wealthy now from property ownership. Many others, who often don't come to church, spent their money on the races and in the pubs are still there but are still living in Housing New Zealand property, still depending on Government handouts.

It is so obvious, you have to be blind not to see it. It is God's blessing on those that love him and work for him. There is no other explanation for it.

One of the many changes to a Tongan Christian who accepts Jesus Christ and lives for him is the involvement in church activities and working as a group. That is where the difference is made. My uncle had established a 'Property Purchasing Group' with his Tongan Methodist Group members. They put in $100 each every month to make a deposit for a house. Every member has a turn and by the end of 12 months, the group would have bought 12 properties. In those days, the deposit for a property was just $2,000 or so and you need just 20 people putting in $100 each for the deposit, every month. Mortgage payments were just $40-$50 a week and very affordable. If you were saving $50 a week to get your $2,000 for the deposit, it will never happen because there are so many things to pay! And 3 years is a long time!

That is just one example of how a group living for Jesus Christ can work together to better each other's lives.

Another example, is funerals. If any church member has a funeral, all the church groups will donate as much as $20-30,000 for the funeral in today's dollars. Any church member who need money for emergencies will go to the Church Minister and ask and God will deliver every time. A fellowship for Christ also works wonders for the members every need.

Such is the blessing, and miracle, of belonging to Christ from my own personal experience.

Chapter 2.

Blessing from a man of God

Many locally famous people came to preach in our new church and one day a locally famous evangelist came. He was somebody whose reputation preceded him. He can heal the sick and inspire people spiritually. Our whole church was abuzz with excitement, I have never seen the church so full and even some people were left outside.

The Minister told us kids a story of a burning ship. An eleven year old boy was told by his father to wait for him on deck while he seek help. Many of the passengers asked the boy to come with them in the small boats but he refused. He says that his father had told him to wait for his return.

It was an example in trust. The preacher said, we should trust God like the little boy trusted his father. He also said, 'Is there anyone here who is eleven years old?'. I put up my hand and he says, 'pay attention at school, come to church, work hard, God has a plan for your life'.

I have been doing very well in Primary School and was awarded the best student prize every term for 20 out of 21 terms I was in Primary School from 1967 to 1973. And I did not think too much about the Minister's words but my life changed dramatically. I passed the national exam and entered Tonga High School at age 12 in 1974. Only the best and brightest students from the whole country went there. I did very well at Tonga High School that I was the only Tongan boy who passed New Zealand School Certificate in 5 subjects in 1978 and again in the University Entrance Examination in 1979. I feel I did not do anything extraordinary to have that outstanding result, but I did! My friend Roger Bernabe, from the Phillipines, was the only other boy who passed in 5 subjects in both years and also 3 of the girls. There were more than 100 students from the local schools sitting the exams. It gave me a kind of Albert Einstein reputation in the local gossip.

It was another miracle!

I have been doing what the evangelist told me some 6 years before. I paid attention at school, I attended church every Sunday and I worked hard in the family plantation.

The plantation

Our church members had a yam and taro garden in one of the parish member's farm about 30 or 40 minutes walk from our house and my Dad usually asked me to go and get some taro from the plantation. He bought me a bicycle when I passed the exam to Tonga High School. I would go on the bicycle with a large 20 kg sack and dig up some taro for our evening meal. We call it taro but it is not colocasia taro. It is cocoyam taro. Cocoyam, also known as xanthosoma, was normally planted in the holes after the yam has been harvested and the yield was good because the ground was soft. My job was to dig out the cormlets that grow from the main cocoyam corm and put them in the sack. Once I have about half a sack it was time to come home.

It was an exercise navigating the bicycle around the potholes on the road with half a 20 kilo sack of cocoyam sitting on the handle bar but I was getting pretty good at it. Some of the potholes were bigger than trucks!

During the mango and lychee season, I would spend some time collecting mangoes from under the trees around the farms. Ripe mangoes fall of the tree and are very sweet. The whole area is covered in bush and so I hardly see anyone. I would also climb the lychees and pick them. I have been reading the stories of Tom Sawyer and Huckleberry Finn at Tonga High School and imagine myself exploring like they did.

Spending time in the bush, taught me a kind of self pride and reliance, just like those mountain men in the American cowboy stories. When I am by myself in the bush harvesting our crop, it gave me a feeling of freedom and control of my destiny. It contributed to my confidence in passing my exams years later, I think.

It started a love of gardening and the farm activities that I ended up working for Agriculture after graduating from university later in life. That early training gave me a 'street wise' outlook and attitude that saw me succeed while others fail.

Being sick and reading books

I also got the measles and dengue fever which grounded me at home for 2 or more weeks each time. I would read every book in my father's chest of books, even his maths and history books while at home. My Mum tells me to stay in my room so I pass the time looking at pictures and reading. By the time I was back at school I had read the entire history of the United States, Great Britain and even the Tongan Bible from cover to cover! I often wonder about it. That started a love of reading that probably inspired me to write so many books today.

Was that another of God's ways of showing me what to do? If I had not become sick and read all those books, I probably would not love reading so much.

Over the years, from 1976 to 1979, my friends had repeatedly led me astray many times, I felt God had kept faith with me and did not let any harm befall me. Why do I say that? Because many of the Tonga High School students have been suspended or expelled from school for similar mischief. Drinking alcohol and smoking cigarettes were the worst offenses.

At the end of 1979, our principal organized a school in Auckland, New Zealand for us to further our studies. Roger and I both grabbed the opportunity with 2 hands. I can feel my parents were very proud that I would further my studies overseas. Dad and my brother had just harvested a plot of Candy Red watermelons with really good results. I helped them sell the melons at the Talamahu Market on the first day. Normally the local growers would pick their melons and bring the load by truck and just heap them on the concrete floor of the market. Three of us were standing around the heap selling and taking the cash. The price starts at 50 cents for small one kilo melons to $5 for the large 10 kilo or bigger melons. We started about 7 am and made about $400 by 3pm. The yearly salary for government first year staff was about $500! So our sale on the first day was pretty good. I got $10 for the days work! That is about a week's wage.

Out of the watermelon sales my Dad gave me $NZ 500 to take with me. I have never had so much money in my pocket and I made sure it lasted the whole year.

Me and Roger both did well at Mt Albert Grammar School and earned enough marks to enter the

University of Auckland and we both graduated with Bachelors of Science in 1985!

That was also a miracle! I even surprised myself when I got my Bachelor of Science. Every kid should remember that, if you aim high and work hard you can succeed. I never thought, at Primary School or even High School, that I would one day have a university degree. We can show the kids now that it is quite achievable, anyone can do it.

I was rather pleased with myself because very few Tongans succeed at University as private students. Most apply for a government scholarship.

I had stayed with my uncle, the Reverend Taniela Moala, who was the Minister of the Tongan Methodist Church of New Zealand. He had just bought a new house at Balmoral, Auckland. I did attend our Methodist Church Service at Dominion Road, and Kingsland, whenever I can. I really enjoyed going to church every Sunday and the fellowship with the Tongan Methodist Church members of my age, especially my cousins.

I worked hard to earn enough money to pay my way through University, because I was a private student. Every summer I would visit Student Job search at Auckland University Student Association building and check the jobs on offer. The AUSA usually do a great job each year. The large office walls were covered with job tickets and we just take the phone number and call them. I usually land a job after 3-4 calls so I feel lucky every time. That job will keep me busy for the whole summer. That was kind of confidence building. I felt that I can always get a job if I want to.

It was a miracle that I always find jobs to save money for the next year. From 1981 to 1984, I found jobs every summer from student job search and even during the year I always find part time jobs. Somehow, I always knew that I can always get a job if I needed one.

That was also a miracle because many university students were not so lucky! I am not sure why, but it was probably preference. I take any job on offer, most local students would have a preference or they would just 'go for a holiday' as many had bursary and scholarships…..and rich parents to cover costs in the next year. They would rather be skiing or do something exotic.

I never ask my uncle or the church for money to help with my university costs. I was perfectly able to pay for them myself. My uncle provide a roof over my head. It was a good house in a wealthy suburb so I was very lucky. He never ask me for any payment although I give some money to my cousin, when I am working, for shopping. I also donated some money for the house renovation.

I usually save about $1,200 to $1,600 every summer and I would still have $200 or so left at the end of the year.

The part time jobs did help during the year and it took the finance pressure off my mind. I was washing dishes and making salads at a Italian Restaurant and was also a Shop Assistant at the biggest shop in town, the Farmers Trading Company at Hobson Street.

The restaurant job was amazing. My boss, the chef makes me dinner every night. I choose any pizza, ravioli, cannelloni, steak and he even have rabbit and venison from his hunting trips. I can have red wine or brandy with my meal then cassata and cheesecake for dessert.

I worked in the Trade Tools Section at Farmers, sometimes in the Garden Section. I learned everything there is to know about tools and how to use them.

As university students we were suckers for a good time. There were always 'booze ups' and parties to go to. I did enjoy having a few drinks with mates and telling a few jokes. I think it is good for a student to go through all that, it was kind of enlightening in a way.

One of my friends did joke that I was a 'wayward student' because of my fondness of alcohol and parties which was frowned upon in the Methodist Church. Alcohol is not allowed at all. Methodist Church members can have tobacco and drink the Tongan *kava* but not alcohol especially if they are lay preachers. Us young men and even some of the girls can sneak off to a few parties.

What I think now is that God's blessing is bestowed upon us without any judgement on our personal performance. In my case for example, I was still blessed as the evangelist told me, even though I had deviated from the 'holy path' into what most Methodists consider the 'path of the devil.' Drinking alcohol, going with women to parties and so on. However, this is a normal phenomenon in the European cultures and most of my student friends were Europeans.

After graduation

I returned to Tonga after graduation from Auckland University and got a job with the Ministry of Agriculture. Then I got a job with the University of the South Pacific and the South Pacific Commission.

In 1993, I was made an expert at two of the United Nation's Expert Panels.

I often wonder about the Minister's prediction. He did open my eyes to a lot of things about religion especially the fellowship he established which is now one of the biggest in Tonga with its own High School and University.

Chapter 3.

A greater path is opened for me

When God does something to change your life, he will make sure you understand it. Here are some examples of how God had made sure his message is clear and understood.

(i) The conversion of Saul to Christianity.

When Jesus chose Saul to be his disciple, Saul had no doubt whatsoever who it is.

In Acts 9: 1-9, Saul's conversion is explained.

'Meanwhile, Saul was still breathing out murderous threats against the Lord's disciples. He went to the high priest and asked him for letters to the synagogues in Damascus, so that if he found any there who belonged to the Way, whether men or women, he might take them as prisoners to Jerusalem. As he neared Damascus on his journey, suddenly a light from

heaven flashed around him. He fell to the ground and heard a voice say to him, "Saul, Saul, why do you persecute me?"

"Who are you, Lord?" Saul asked.

"I am Jesus, whom you are persecuting," he replied. "Now get up and go into the city, and you will be told what you must do."

The men traveling with Saul stood there speechless; they heard the sound but did not see anyone. Saul got up from the ground, but when he opened his eyes he could see nothing. So they led him by the hand into Damascus. For three days he was blind, and did not eat or drink anything.

Saul was totally blind and scared. But he was saved by one of the Christian followers, Ananias as Jesus had directed. Saul was converted. He went on to become the most influential of all the disciples of Christ. It is said, he changed his name to Paul because he is now a follower of Christ. The name Saul of Tarsus is a Hebrew name but the name Paul is a Roman equivalent. Somehow Paul's Roman citizenship is a very good influence on his life. It saved him from certain death once and also helped him spread the gospel as he was preaching mostly to the gentiles.

(ii) The selection of Jonah

Jonah was commanded by God to go and preach against Nineveh, a great city which has become wicked in its ways. But Jonah was afraid and he ran away to Tarshish on a boat. God send a storm so great the boat crew had no choice but to throw Jonah into the sea, when it was discovered he was the cause. God send a great fish to swallow Jonah who survived for 3 days and 3 nights inside the fish, before he repented and the fish took him to dry land.

God commanded Jonah again to go to Niniveh and preach against their sinful ways and Jonah obeyed this time.

There are many other examples in the Bible of how God had changed people's lives and given them a new direction.

The 12 chosen disciples of Jesus are also examples of how God used them for his purpose. They became empowered by Jesus Christ to become leaders of men and even though they were persecuted and killed, the church survived to take over the Roman Empire itself.

(iii) What God did for me

What happened to me, I have no doubt, saved me from a very different life. God had closed one door and opened a better one.

Here is what happened.

When I entered Form 5 at Tonga High School, in 1978, I had been playing rugby since Primary School and it was my ambition to play in the Tonga High School First 15 in the next year, 1979. I joined the Grade 5 team in 1978 to prepare myself for a First 15 spot the following year.

I was given the left wing as I was a bit faster than most of my team mates. We played our first game at the main stadium number two field in town called the Teufaiva Stadium. The other team were from a school notorious for putting in bigger boys in their teams, to give them an advantage, in order to win. It is called grade 5 because only boys with certain weights are allowed to play in the grade.

The very first ball I got at full speed as we started an attack from about half way, I got hit by two very big guys and I must have passed out. I woke up, probably a few minutes later, the game was on the other side of the field. I can feel a searing pain on my left side. I tried to stand up and noticed my left hand was hanging lower than my right. The pain on my left shoulder was unbelievable. I used my right hand to hold up my left and walked outside the field. The Coach came over and asked me what happened. I told him my shoulder is probably dislocated and I should go home and seek help. He agreed.

In Tonga at that time, there were no ambulances or medics to help injured rugby players. I just have to walk home holding my injured side. It took about 40 minutes of unbelievable painful 'leg movements' to get home. I say 'leg movements' because I was in a daze and I am just putting one foot in front of the other.

My Mum took me to the local chiropractor who tried to 'correct the bone'. It was a trip on foot of about 1 hour to the traditional healer's house. We had to stop many times on the way so I can rest. The buses normally don't operate in the evening and in 1978 there were only 4 taxis in the whole town, so walking was the only option.

To make a long story short, I did go to the hospital the next day and got x rayed. They told me my collar bone is broken and showed me the x ray film. The Doctor advised that its best to let it heal naturally. I was given a piece of calico to hold my hand up and nature will do the rest.

Even though getting around was uncomfortable, I was getting used to it.

I did not play any more rugby that year (1978) and the following year (1979). I spent more time studying, as I was not playing rugby, and I was the only boy to pass in 5 subjects in both the New Zealand School Certificate (1978) and University Entrance (1979) Exams. It was simply amazing. I can imagine how proud my parents and family were. It was the major impetus that gave me courage and confidence to continue my studies in New Zealand.

Our school Principal, Mr Viliami Fukofuka, had arranged for us to attend Form 7 at Mt Albert Grammar School in Auckland, New Zealand. It was a huge step up for me. Arriving at Auckland airport and looking at the farms around the area gave me an idea that it is a totally different landscape to the one I am used to in Tonga.

I can see miles and miles of farmland. Only the sea was that big in the islands.

Again, I tried for the Mt Albert Grammar School First 15. I got hit, again, on the same collarbone that broke 2 years before. It was so sore I was scared it might be broken again! I quit rugby again that year and spent my time studying and I passed, with enough marks, to enter the University of Auckland in 1981.

I think if I did not get injured playing rugby in 1978 and got into the First 15, I would have got carried away with it and failed my exams. It is well known, to all the students, how the First 15 boys drink alcohol, after games on Friday, and generally get into mischief because of it as they usually do things as a group. Many of the THS old boys are so proud and supportive of the First 15 team wins, they provide large amounts of alcohol and cash for the boys. Our 1979 first 15 team was so good they were in the final but lost to St Johns High School.

The fact that I got injured, again in 1980 at Mt Albert Grammar, makes it very clear that God is closing the rugby door for me. At the University of Auckland, I did play rugby again and we became champions in the local competition in 1982, but I graduated with a Bachelor of Science. I was mature enough to handle all the after matches and problems that come my way.

I have no doubts now, if rugby was for me I would have played for the Tonga National Team. I returned to Tonga in June 1985 and got a job with MAFF and started training with a local team. I managed to play two games at Teufaiva Stadium but because I travel so much, for work meetings and trainings, I gave up the rugby.

In 1997, I went on to do a Master of Science with Honours, at the University of Auckland. Two years later, I got a good job with the University of the South Pacific in Samoa. After one and a half years I applied and got a job a better job with the South Pacific Commission (SPC is now known as the Secretariat for the Pacific Community) in Fiji.

In total, I spent 10 years in the Pacific Islands and travelled to more than 20 countries around the world during that time, as a Scientist. I was even an expert in two of the United Nations expert panels at the Food and Agriculture Organization in Rome, Italy.

I decided to migrate with my family to New Zealand in 1996 after my first contract with SPC.

I remembered the words of the evangelist, some 48 years from that sermon long ago in a small church in Tonga and I began to wonder. After studying the scriptures and other literature for my book series called GOD IS ENERGY. DO YOU BELIEVE?, I began to think about it.

The more I see what is happening around me and the world and interpreting it in light of what I have written in my 5 books in the God is Energy series, I have no doubt that God's hand has guided me all these years since I was a child. Like the story of the footprints on the sand, I can see only one set of footprints on the sand these past 48 years. Jesus has been carrying me like a lost sheep in his arms. The words of the evangelist did come true.

God did have a plan for my life. I now realize that I am in the enviable position of understanding God from a scientific point of view. I believe that God wants me to write all that information down so others can read about it.

Like so many people who experienced and spoke of their OBEs and NDEs, I know that I have a greater purpose to fulfil. That is a miracle in itself, because I can see where it is all going. I am becoming more and more experienced in understanding life after death that I can help explain to others. Like all the stories related in those OBEs and NDEs, I feel I have that understanding, I am one with the knowledge and I am one with the infinite. Maybe that is what they mean by being enlightened as in the case of Buddha. He had to search for it himself. I have the benefit of reading about it from the stories of so many other people.

That is the miracle of modern technology and knowledge, you can learn and do all those things that took a lifetime to discover, in just a few days or weeks by reading the works of others.

Chapter 4.

Always First in Class

When I started Primary School, in 1967 at Longolongo Primary School in Nuku'alofa, Kingdom of Tonga, the buildings were made of coconut thatch and wood from the local bush area. The floor was still bare ground covered in coconut fronds and coconut frond mats. It wasn't until 1968 or 1969 that we had brick, louvre and corrugated iron long houses build. I can still remember sitting on the concrete floor at the end of each term for the prize giving ceremony. It was a big occasion for us students as we will not be coming back to school for two weeks and at the end of the year, almost 3 months!

I was not expecting anything special. I was just like any student but I was surprised every time that my name is always called last.

Normally, each teacher of every class starting from Class 1 and finishing with Class 6, would come up to the front and call out the names of his or her students according to how they performed starting with the 'last in the class' and finishing with the 'Captain of the Class' at number 1. And every term, starting from Class 1 I was always the last to be called. 'And the Captain of the Class is Semisi Pule'. I would get up and walk to the front where I receive a prize as Captain or 'First in Class'. It was usually a parcel containing some exercise books and pencils with a rubber. It means I don't have to buy any exercise books or pens in the next term or year.

I was wondering why I was always first in class, I did not feel any different or belong to the nobility, the aristocrats of the country. I wasn't special at all, I walk barefoot to school and I wear the same uniform as everybody but I was always first in class!

I understood it one day when our father decided to test me against my older brother. My father would read out certain words for us to spell and mathematics, additions, divisions or multiplications for us to complete. My older brother is 5 years older than me. I was in Primary School in Class 5 while he was in High School in Form 3 or 4. I was about 11 years old and he was 16 years of age.

It came as a huge shock when I realize that I can beat my brother in that simple test. When my father took our pieces of paper and checked our spelling and maths answers, I spelled all the words correctly and did all the mathematics questions correctly. My brother made some mistakes and got some answers wrong!

I realize then that I have a gift! I know how to spell the words correctly and do the maths questions too. So I took it for granted that I am the best student in our class and the best student at school with more than 100 students. I know how to answer the questions correctly and the others could not. That is why I was always first in class.

Maybe the Church Minister was right, God does have a plan for me. Looking back now, I was first in class for 20 terms out of 21. In my last year, before leaving for High School, I was second in class.

I heard the reason was, I had decided to 'miss some of the dance practice' for the school competition.

There was a dance competition for all the schools and one of my friends persuaded me to 'run away' with him and another mate. The dance our school was learning was called a '*lakalaka*' which has up to a hundred or more performers in it. Our Principal wanted to win the competition and so any student missing practice were punished. We were missed and punished. I also got dropped from 'first in class' to 'second in class' in that last year. That was a good lesson for me, I should never listen to those who are not as smart as me. I should make decisions myself.

There were a few cases of that.

> Never let those less smarter than you persuade you to get into trouble.

Our school did win the competition against the traditional powerhouses in the *lakalaka*. We wore traditional costume and I could feel while performing that we were pretty good. Our dance lyrics was also very inspiring being composed by no less than the Crown Princes's Talking Chief. We beat the traditional powers in the *lakalaka* dance which were the villages of Mu'a and Kolovai.

It seems odd, looking back 47 years later, but I have a feeling somebody was helping our side to win.

Probably the same person who build the church next door and the same person who took me to the best school! And the same person who took me to Auckland University and around the world as a Scientist!

Was it my destiny to be the writer of these books? To proclaim the gospel in a new light, to explain the trinity in scientific terms?

I have a feeling we are on the verge of discovering time and space travel, not based on spaceships but based on the definition of God!

Chapter 5

Encounters with a parallel Universe

I want to relate these stories to give the reader some idea of the kind of experiences I have had. Because of my background and also what I have read and written, about God and the Devil, I have a very alert disposition to these phenomena which most people may dismiss as 'just one of those things' or just natural occurrences that cannot be explained.

The problem for me is that, it happens too many times to be ignored and like in a statistical test, it is highly significant.

Energy black hole?

Yesterday, Saturday 19 of September 2020, I went to my garden in the Waikato region of the North Island of New Zealand. I wanted to finish a deck I was building for the summer lunches and hopefully visits by the family. I breed watermelons and also grow plantain and taro. I had just bought 2 packets of screws from Bunnings Warehouse and wanted to finish binning the deck floor boards. After about 10 minutes, the cordless drill battery ran out of power. I decided to call somebody and tried using my brand new Samsung Galaxy, its battery also ran out of power. Coincidence? Maybe. Something sucked the energy out of the batteries.

The funny thing was I heard a strange noise as if it was a bird laughing!

Normally there would be two fantails flitting around between the shrubs as if they are happy to see me, but they were no where to be seen. Kereru or local pigeons visit but none to be seen.

I heard the beast

When I was building the tool shed, in my garden, in March 2018, a man came and visited and just before I saw him I distinctly heard a voice. It came from down the valley. It sounded like gibberish from an alien. The kind you hear in alien movies. I actually heard that same voice many years before when I was still working for the South Pacific Commission in Fiji! And the man I saw? It was the Human Resources Manager for the South Pacific Community. He said he wanted to meet my friend, but when I asked my friend. He said, he does not know him! Strange!

I was building the shed for storage of my tools so I don't have to bring them every time. My car is a Peugeot 206 which does not have much room for taking a lot of tools and other bits and pieces. I have had much problems with rats probably because of the stuff stored in the shed, they use for bedding and so on. The shed smelled of rats all the time even though I use rat bait every week.

Strangely yesterday, it really hit me that the shed does not smell of rats anymore! The rats seem to have vacated the premises. It smelled really clean!

When the drill and phone ran out juice, my immediate thought was, did something scare the rats away?

The Beast

The voices I heard in Fiji and also in the Waikato seemed to me to sound very similar to the beast that roared at our house in Northcote, Northshore of Auckland.

I also have a weird sensation that it is the same entity that broke down the computer when I was writing the first book 'God is Energy. Do you Believe?'. And the same one that picked up a ladder and threw it at my car last year!

Here's how it happened.

I was given a small contracts job to do at a large unoccupied house. I went up the first morning and park my Peugeot 206, beside the house, opened the boot and started unloading. I had brought a 2 meter ladder with me tied to the roof and I had put it about 5 meters away after taking it off. Then suddenly, a very strong gust of wind picked up the ladder and threw it at my car hitting it just behind the left front lights. I was a bit shocked at first but got over it. I took some pictures then painted the scratch over to prevent any rust setting in.

Just a few weeks ago I was looking for some pictures then come across the picture I took of the scratch on the car, about a year ago. It really shocked me beyond belief. The scratch looks like a beast was smiling at me! A distinct row of front 7 small incisors in the middle and two prominent fang like incisors teeth like the upper teeth of a carnivore! Then it hit me, the sudden gust of wind and the sensation that somebody is saying something gibberish.

Here's the picture;

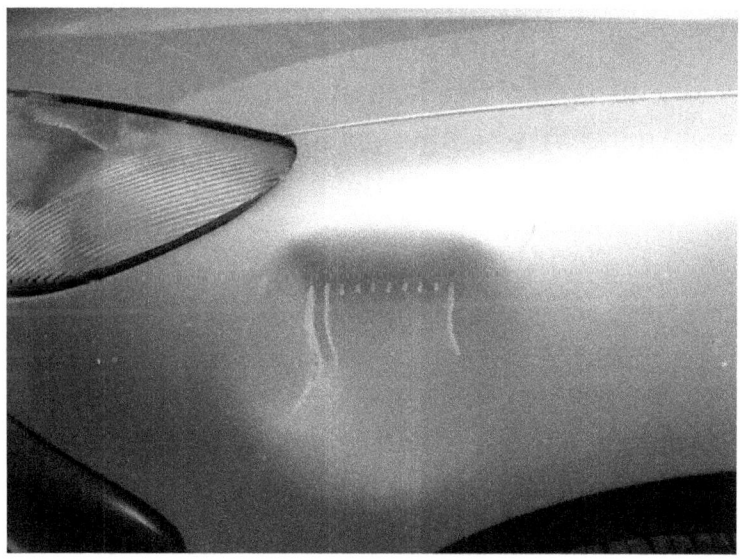

I am normally not scared because I am getting used to it, but I am beginning to wonder.

I checked the front teeth of carnivores, on google, and the closest animal to this imprint is a tiger. A bear has 6 small incisor teeth, a dog has 5, a lion has 5 and a tiger has 7 which is the same as the imprint on my car! Animals may have different numbers of teeth according to species and age and so on but on the pictures I found on google only the tiger had 7 incisor teeth between its fangs.

What significance does a tiger showing his upper teeth on my car have? Most people will just say it is a 'coincidence' but I think not, there are too many coincidences it becomes a cluster. In my statistical inference mind, it is highly significant and therefore caused by 'something' as in the case of viruses spreading in the field!

Here's something that will blow your mind and I think it maybe the case.

Because of my great interest in life and death and the possibility of souls travelling through space to another solar system or galaxy, I have unwittingly opened a star gate like in the movies. Just like when you pray you welcome the Holy Spirit to help you. Through that star gate, monsters or beings from another realm comes through in an instant but my 'inner being' is a very strong self as the apostle John pointed out.

The one inside me is stronger.

I always feel a kind of inner resistance when these phenomena occurs as if I am willing the monster back to where it came from, as if I am throwing it back through the star gate with my willpower.

It is the same every time, somehow, the one inside me kicks the monster back to its own origin but it keeps coming back!

In OBE and NDE experiences, we can tell the spirit world as unfolding in the stories of patients and people who have been there, is a much more real world than ours. But it is still outside the gates, once the spirit goes through the gate, there is no coming back. We have not seen or heard from anyone who has been through the gate.

This spiritual phenomena I am experiencing is proof that there are other dimensions or realms and sometimes we can have momentary experience that shows a glimpse of those worlds. Suppose the monster who attacked my car had won?

What would become of me? Would the monster devour me and take my spirit back with it to this other realm?

I have always known since I was a little boy that God is always with me, even when I don't go to church or get involved in any religious activity. Maybe the monster was just challenging God for my spirit? Or whatever it wanted from me?

You can tell from my stories that it has happened many times and God wins all the time. If the beast wins, that will be the end of my life on this earth, I think.

I heard the beast roar

When I was writing the first book of the 'God is Energy. Do you Believe?' series my computer kept breaking down so many times I decided to go to the library and use their computer. Then about 12 pm I returned home to make some lunch and also watch the 12 pm news. I turned on the TV in the living room then went into the adjacent kitchen to make a sandwich. Suddenly, there was a clap of thunder so loud and violent it shook our house for several seconds. It sounded to me like the roar of the monster in the movie Godzilla. I was still shaking when I noticed the thunder had stopped and the TV was on!

I kept thinking to myself, what are the chances of that happening as a natural event?

For my Master of Science degree I did a lot of statistical tests and inferences about a virus disease of vanilla in the Kingdom of Tonga. It was part of a study of the epidemiology of the disease. I am very familiar with random and clustered distribution statistical tests. A random distribution means that it is just a natural event, but when you have a cluster of diseased plants, 'something' is causing it to happen and therefore it is not a natural phenomenon.

Using that same logic frame, I can tell that many of the events I have witnessed are probably not natural or random. 'Something' is causing them to occur. They are not random but clusters.

The spirit in the lab

One incident was probably the most scary in most of my experiences. One night, in 1988, while I was working in the Biological Science Plant Pathology Lab at the University of Auckland, I distinctly felt a presence in the lab. I was trying to finish some experiments for my Master of Science Thesis and some of the experiments require many hours and late nights. I got up and checked all the rooms in the lab. The supervisor's room, the storage room, the other lab, technician's room and prep room but I see no one. It was about 10 pm at night and I was feeling a bit scared. The sensation that somebody is there with me was so strong!

I decided to go home so I turned off the lights in the lab and locked it. I went down to the ground floor and also locked the main door, then left.

Next day, about 9 am I arrived by bus and walked down Symond Street in the middle of the campus. I met one of my mate's son from our University Squash Team and asked him how his Dad was doing. The kid started crying and said his Dad died the night before at about the same time I had that sensation of a 'presence' in the lab! He had a massive heart attack!

I have had several sensations like that in different situations and places, like my experiences with the gibberish and 'beast', but not as strong as the one in the laboratory and also collaborated by the son of the diseased.

Even the cordless drill and phone losing power made the hair on my neck stand out. It was so pronounced I have a feeling there is a presence around me. It is probably the large amount of 'experiences' I have had that makes it less 'traumatic' because I am just 'getting used to it'. I just get on with my work and ignore it.

As I point out in the book, the Antichrist, the apostle John wrote about it 2,000 years ago.

In 1 John 4:4 he says;

'the one inside you is stronger than the one out there'

It gives me strength and power over anything that is 'out there'. I can feel it. I am the master and it will obey me if I command it to leave, just like Jesus Christ pointed out in Matthew 21:21.

"For truly I tell you, if you have faith the size of a mustard seed, you can say to this mountain, 'Move

from here to there,' and it will move. Nothing will be impossible for you."

The painful hands and feet

I have been suffering from gout like pain for several years, probably since 2012 when I went to my Mum's funeral!. About February 2015, I went to Tonga, again, on a trip to collect pictures and information for my books.

It was a simple plan, I just walked all over Nuku'alofa taking pictures then go to the MAFF Research Library and collect some information from there.

Then one time I walked through the Cemetery known as Telekava on the western side of Nuku'alofa. I took some pictures around the Cemetery and also some photos beside the graves, mostly of flowering weeds. I distinctly felt that some people are watching me. It is a very old cemetery and I have been walking around there, as a child. Several relatives are buried there, including my grandfather and older brother.

The camera battery ran out of steam so I came back to my aunties house, where I stayed, to charge up the camera battery. The next morning my whole body was in agony as if something has taken over it. I remember watching the Men in Black movie starring Will Smith and Tommy Lee Jones about an alien cockroach which took over a human body. That is exactly how it felt, I was suddenly unable to walk.

Somebody brought some crutches but I was barely able to use it. My hands and feet seem to refuse to cooperate and it was very, very painful.

My gout medicine from New Zealand had run out and I was taking panadol. It was the only medicine I can get from the shops. I was well enough to go to the Vaiola hospital, one day, and got some gout medicine but still the pain persisted.

Miraculously, one of my nieces came one morning. Her name is Mo'ui. It means 'to live, to have life' in the Tongan language and I asked her to please go and get some panadol for me, I had run out of medicine again. She bought the panadol from the Chinese shop next door and I started taking them. The next morning all the pain was gone! As if I was not sick at all!

I booked my return ticket to New Zealand and left in a hurry. I got the right medicine from my Doctor and I was well enough to go walking again after so many weeks! I normally enjoy a 2-3 hour walk once a week or so especially on the beach from Takapuna to Milford or at Mission Bay.

Whatever got into me in Tonga, I have no doubt was an unfriendly 'entity'. It seem to leave me alone when the girl (Mo'ui) came I asked her to help me! Its as if the unfriendly spirit agreed with my request for some help from Mo'ui!

The shaking house

When both my parents have passed, I stayed at their house at the suburb of Tu'atakilangi in Nuku'alofa when I visit Tonga to collect information. At night the place is so dark and the air so 'thick', it is almost like a chocolate cake, I can just cut it with a knife. When you are in a place like Auckland where there is hardly a dark spot at night, you can appreciate the 'darkness' in Tonga where there is hardly any street lights in most areas outside the main CBD. The sky looks so amazing with the starlight the only light you can see.

In addition, my parent's electricity supply had been disconnected because there is no one staying at the house. I was just using candles and a battery operated lamp. At night I always have this feeling that the rocks underneath the house are moving and the house seem to sway a little bit even a slight murmur of a shake. I did not pay it much attention, I thought they were just small earthquakes.

Tonga had a massive 7.2 earthquake in 1977 which damaged many buildings and so many after tremors that we know earthquakes very well. I was sleeping at home during that earthquake and I woke up when the bed keep hitting the walls as if a violent person is shaking it. I just found out next morning it was an earthquake. In fact, the biggest Tonga ever had. There was also a pronounced sound like the breaking of the surf on the reef. No one really worked out what caused the sound. I have also heard many tornadoes and the terrible sound it makes seem similar.

I had the shock of my year when my sister told me the former tenants in our parent's house had left because they complain about the house shaking every night! I dare not tell her that I also experienced the house shaking at night when I was there on my own for 3 months! I simply ignored the shaking and went to sleep!

Was it a poltergeist? Like they have in the movies?

My cousin saw our dead Grandfather waving at him

One of my cousins stayed with us in town to attend Queen Salote College. It was often the case that many of my cousins from my parent's village would stay with us to save bus money and only go home in the weekends.

She had a heart condition. She was very brave about it and we did not want to remind her or anybody that she is sick but we knew one day she will probably die of it. And she did die when she was in her late teens. We all went to the village to attend the funeral. We were all very sad, but it was expected.

During the ʻapo which is the last night with the dead before they are buried according to Tonga culture, there is usually singing of hymns and lots of crying and wailing.

We were sitting in an old copra drying house opposite the main house where the funeral took place. I was sitting above in the dryer tray, with the kids, while the older men sat around the bottom at the front of the dryer. It was dark but a 100 watt light bulb in front of the house showed the main door. Most of the men were uncles and several cousins too, just talking about the family and the funeral. The dead girl's brother suddenly shakes and cries out in a very unusual shaky tone.

He says,

'Look, looook'

And everyone was quiet and looked at him. He was pointing at the door of the main house. He says our grandfather is waving at him to come inside the house! It is a common phenomenon in Tongan funerals that many of the relatives claim to see a few dead people attending the funeral!

In many cases the person affected would get up and run off into the dark night. Everyone are always too scared to follow and usually they find the person asleep at the local cemetery the next day! The usual story they tell was that a dead relative asked him to come there!

In the last section on reincarnation and OBE, NDE experiences we can see that those experiences people have of the supernatural is a very common occurrence all over the world.

Avatars

In Hinduism, they believe that the Gods sometime take on human form to help humans by being teachers. Teaching humans how to live and how to raise their children, what to eat, how to fish, grow and raise crops and animals for food and so on. Even the philosophy of life like what they believe in Hinduism and Buddhism, written in ancient scriptures to preserve them for all time.

Just like Jesus Christ is a human form of God in Christianity. Jesus, as God, came to earth to teach man how to receive God and live a holy life on earth.

He also showed mankind that after they die, they can rise from the dead and return to God the Father in heaven. When Jesus left the earth, he send God the Holy Spirit to be man's guide, and helper, for ever.

These human forms are called Avatars, in Hinduism and Buddhism, just like in the James Cameron movie of that same name. A human takes on another form while he is asleep and that other form or body lives in a different realm or parallel universe. What happens when that other body also exist on earth? It would cause a problem obviously because there is only one spirit with 2 bodies.

But from the same idea, we can deduce that other strong spirits can also take on human form to cause problems on earth or for people they don't like for whatever reason.

When somebody says something really nasty to you next time, you can consider it a spirit from another realm attacking you. Just like an Avatar can take on a human form to cause good or teach humans. I think that evil spirits can penetrate the wall between the two worlds and attack humans on earth.

In Hinduism, for example there is a belief that everything we do is being recorded in the cosmos. Just like a computer stores files, every word, every thought, every action is stored in the cosmos. This file is what causes karma, it is the force driving the cycle of death and rebirth. If you happen to be good you come back as a human. If you were less than good, you might reincarnate as a cockroach! You get demoted in the divine scheme of things.

It is a very interesting philosophy because it really makes the point that the 'true self' is not the human body but the spirit! And the spirit is trying to escape this 'unsatisfactory existence' on earth and return to the Cosmic Spirit or God.

It is exactly the same proposition in Christianity, Buddhism and Islam. The true self is the spirit, not the body. The spirit is the eternal one and it wants to return to God where it comes from. Somehow, it was relegated to a lesser existence on earth which is a painful and poor form of itself.

It appears that most religions have the same idea in mind. The goal of this life is to return to God in heaven or paradise after we die.

Unfortunately, although we now know more about life after death, no one has gone through the gates and come back to tell us about it. Most OBEs and NDEs only speak of a brief moment in that other world before being met by dead relatives and friends and told to come back, their purpose in life has not been fulfilled. They are told that if they proceed there will be no return. But what they tell us thus far seem to corroborate what Jesus Christ proposes. Even the other religions have a similar idea. The details of being Christian, Hindu, Buddhist or Moslem maybe different, but they all propose the same thing. Eternal life of the spirit after death of the earthly body.

PART II

THE HOLY TRINITY

Chapter 1

The Trinity

In the Christian Bible there are many references to the trinity. Trinity means three, God in three persons, God the Father, God the Son and God the Holy Spirit. Some writers are now using the term Tri-Unity which means Trinity, but is clearer, in meaning to the reader.

In Matthew 28:19, Jesus said;

Therefore go and make disciples of all nations, baptizing them in the name of the Father and of the Son and of the Holy Spirit.

This is what the Christian churches talk about as the Trinity. God in three persons. Since that commandment to his disciples, in Matthew 28:19, about half the people of the Earth have been converted. To-day, 2,000 years later, 2.52 billion people are recorded to be in the Christian Kingdom, according to official figures. Just over 50%, in the 2.52 billion figure, of Christians still belong to the original universal church (catholics), the rest belong to many groups that have sprung up or broken away from the original universal church.

> **Note**
>
> The Christian Kingdom as referred to in the Bible is what we know as the Catholic Church today. The Pope being the head or monarch of the faith. The Catholic Church was originally called the Universal Church but has broken into two during the wars with the rising influence of Islam in the eleventh century. On one side is the Roman Catholic Church and it is known as the Eastern Orthodox Church on the other. Islam has taken over the middle part of the known world during that time.
>
> Since the rise of protestanism and the anglicans, the modern view of the Christian Kingdom is now more widely applied. Jesus Christ or God is now the head or monarch of the faith and all churches outside the Catholic and Eastern Orthodox are included in the Christian Kingdom.
>
> It should be noted also that Queen Elizabeth II is the Head of the Church of England also known as the Anglican Church. Another monarch as Head of a Christian Organization, but the Church of England considers itself essentially a part of the Universal Church.

Although records show only 2.52 billion Christians on Earth, I believe the number to be much higher. In

New Zealand, for example the government statistics shows 37% to be Christians and 63% to be non-Christian. However, 48.6% of non-Christians have stated they do not belong to any religion. That will include people like myself who do not actively participate in church or religious activities but does attend church services once in a while. Most of those 48.6% are descendant of Christians who are no longer active in church like myself. Some of them, like me, believe is something more than the churches can offer at this time. You can tell from most of my books on Christianity that I include evolution, karma, nirvana and other ideas in my 'Christian theory'. I think there is much more to Jesus Christ than what we have in the Christian Bible.

When I talk about the Christian Kingdom, I am talking about the citizens of the earth who have heard of the message of Christ and believe in it. That message of faith, hope, love, charity and spiritual salvation. I call them the 'five pillars of Christ'. Most New Zealanders practice the 'five pillars of Christ' even though they are not active in a church. If we use New Zealand as the basis for our extrapolation we can extend the number of Christians, on Earth, by another 48.6% to 85.6%.

Doing a little arithmetic we can say, if 37% equals 2.52 billion people then 37% plus 48.6% equals 85.6% or 6.5484% people in the world population are practicing the five pillars of Christ but are not active in a Church. That will leave about 1-1.5 billion people outside the 'five pillars of Christ'. These calculations are based on the 2018 population of the Earth being 7.65 billion. Those citizens of the world who have not heard of the message of Christ are the minority.

It must be noted that Jesus Christ is considered by Moslems as one of their prophets, therefore the 1.5 billion members of Islam would have heard the teachings of Christ already practising the 5 pillars of Christ. They are included in the 6.5 billion members of the Christian Kingdom. It should also be noted that there are variations in ideas among the various Christian churches themselves. Differences in ideas with Islam, for example, is a bit bigger but the principles remain the same. Ideas of how we worship, how we should behave as Christians, what we wear, how we raise our families and so on vary between the churches but the principles or five pillars of Christ will remain the same.

The 3 manifestations of God, God the Father, God the Son and God the Holy Spirit.

Water exist in 3 states in nature, solid ice, liquid and gas or steam. The state of the water depends on the temperature, when it is low, water turns to ice or solid, if it is normal water is a liquid and when it is hot, water turns into steam or act like a gas.

If we think of God the trinity as like the water then we are close to understanding it. There is just one God but three manifestations of it. However, unlike water which is controlled by its surrounding temperature, God's existence or manifestation depend only on the will of God.

In all my books on the 'God is Energy' series, I propose that God is the totality of the universe. The essence of its existence. There are some very important inherent characteristics of God. Not only the trinity but also the explanation of matter.

I have explained in the first book what Albert Einstein proposed in his theory of relativity. Einstein did not include God in his theory. He was a Scientist and in science, the rule of empirical evidence is supreme.

Logic and theory are only part of the whole. But in Einstein's theory we can also see the relationship between God the Father and God the Son and God the Holy Spirit. How is that possible? Just like the manifestations of water when energy is applied to it. The beauty of Einstein's theory of relativity is that it is supported by empirical evidence....and it has nothing to do with religion.

Just to remind us, Einstein's theory is expressed as;

$E = mc^2$

E is energy, m is mass and c is the velocity of light in a vacuum or 300,000 kilometers per second.

The idea of 'God is Energy' as proposed in my books is based on Einstein's Theory of Relativity. In other words God is also mc^2. What does that mean? The equation actually explains the relationship between energy and matter. It basically says that energy and matter are interchangeable! In other words, matter can appear and disappear! Just like the water, it can be solid or ice one minute and changes into steam the next minute. As we all know, the steam disappears into the air!

However, in Einstein's equation the added ingredient is the velocity of light. It basically points out that as you approach the speed of light, matter changes into energy. When you slow down, matter returns to its solid state.

How does that explain God? How can Einstein's equation throw light on our understanding of God?

Here's the end result of Einstein's theory, the atomic bomb. The atomic bomb has so much power it boggles the mind, but all that power comes from a small amount of unstable matter which reacts and release its stored energy in an instant, creating the huge power and devastation of the atomic bomb.

Now, imagine if you can control that power. It can be used for good purposes like electricity production, jet propulsion for our spaceships and much more.

Suppose there is intelligence in that energy, it can change and effect countless miracles in our universe? Who holds the stars and the planets inside the galaxies? Who moves them around in space? Have you ever wondered why something as heavy as the earth is floating in space? Why the sun and the rain provide life with sustenance on earth?

We can see that God is the total energy of the universe, the power of the atomic bomb, controlled into a thing of beauty. There is a scientific law which explains it. It says;

'Energy cannot be created nor destroyed, it can only be changed from one form into another'.

This scientific law is called 'The First Law of Thermodynamics or The Law of Conservation of Energy'.

That explains God the Father! God cannot be created or destroyed, it can only be changed from one form into another.

How does that work?

In Einstein's equation, we are being given empirical evidence that energy and matter are interchangeable. In other words, God the Father which is energy can become God the Son (Jesus Christ) which is matter of flesh and blood. The secret ingredient is the velocity of light. In other words, the mass has to be in motion to become energy and it reverts to mass when the motion stops. But what is the essence of velocity?

The equation for speed is;

$S = d/t$ where S is speed, d is distance and t is time

Speed is equal to distance over time. For velocity it is expressed as;

$V = s/t$ where V is velocity, s is displacement and t is for time

Displacement is more or less equivalent to distance.

Einstein had also proposed, that as you approach the velocity of light, time comes to a stop! I explained his 'Twin Paradox' in the first book of 'God is Energy' series.

It means that when God is in the energy state, time does not exist. That is empirical evidence that God as energy has neither beginning nor end. But God the Son who is flesh and blood will age as we know from the bible because he was born and he died on the cross as flesh and blood. There was a beginning and end to God the Son. That is how we can differentiate between the two. But we all know from the Bible that the legacy of God the Son, his words will never die.

As God the Son says in Matthew 24:35;

'Heaven and earth will pass away, but My words will never pass away.'

Here's the most amazing revelation about the word.

In John 1: 1-5 there is a glimpse of the power of the word;

'In the beginning was the word and the word was with God and the word was God. The same was in the beginning with God. All things were made by him; and without him was not any thing made that was made. In him was life; and the life was the light of men. The light shines in the darkness, but the darkness had not understood it.'

We can see the purpose of this manifestation of God. The five pillars of Christ has helped shape the history of mankind for the past 2,000 years and will continue to shape the human race forever.

Do we have empirical evidence to explain God the Holy Spirit?

As in our water example and as explained by scientific theory, it is possible for God to manifest itself in various forms. The Law of the Conservation of energy gives us a clue.

Here are some examples;

1. Wind energy can be harnessed and changed to (i) electricity (ii) can be used to lift aircraft (iii) propel boats (iv) drive windmills and a million other uses.
2. Electrical energy can be used to (i) revive the dead in the hospitals (ii) create light (iii) drive engines (iv) create heat and so on.

I want to draw our attention to the use of electricity to revive the dead in the hospitals. Why does the dead body of a human respond to electrical currents and become alive again?

When the body was dead, it had all the parts intact but it is still dead! There is a missing ingredient which give it life! What shall we call this ingredient?

In many stories of 'out of body experiences' (OBE) and 'near death experiences' (NDE) by people who died in the hospitals and in accidents, we can get a glimpse of what is going on. Some stories say they were floating near the ceiling of the room and looking down on their dead body on the bed! They saw the Doctors trying to revive them, and then suddenly they wake up again as a human body on the bed.

This is empirical evidence that there is a missing ingredient which gives the dead human body the life it requires. This is what we call the soul or spirit of a person. Most Christians believe when we die, our soul goes to heaven or hell but in some cases the soul does not want to leave and can be 'attracted' back to its body using electrical currents. The soul or spirit is part of the Holy Spirit. All of the belief of the major religions of Christianity, Islam, Hinduism and Buddhism are connected to God the Holy Spirit. It is best summed up as man's effort on earth is to be saved and return to God or the Cosmic spirit.

The Hindu and Buddhist idea are much clearer. All the actions that devotees do on Earth is to achieve a state of enlightenment which will allow them to return to the Cosmic Spirit or they will continue to be reborn or reincarnated into a sinful, painful world as punishment.

The Christian Equivalent is using the 5 pillars of Christ to achieve a state of holiness in Christ and salvation to join God in heaven. The alternative for wickedness is burning in hell.

Islam also believe in the same salvation but through faith and following the teachings of the Prophet Muhammad one enters paradise. The wicked will also be burned in hell with many gates for every wrongdoing.

All these actions by humans are for 'reconnections' of one's spirit or soul with the Holy Spirit.

> *We do not have much scientific evidence to support the idea of hell, although punishment or consequences of sin can be easily recognized.*

Using our scientific examples we can have great confidence, with scientific empirical support, that God the Father, God the Son and God the Holy Spirit do exist as manifestations of the one God.

The idea of God is Energy is clear. Here are the main points;

1. Time does not exist when God is Energy, there is no beginning or end,
2. It does suggest that our Scientific Theory of the Big Bang should be examined in light of this revelation,
3. God is omniscient and omnipotent,
4. God the Son and God the Holy Spirit are manifestations of God, also referred to as God the Father,
5. The manifestations of God depend only on God's will,
6. The manifestation of God the Son teaches humans a guideline for spiritual development, the 5 pillars of Christ,
7. The manifestation of God the Holy Spirit gives mankind an eternal spiritual future,
8. God does reveal his will through human progress,
9. God is actively involved in human affairs,

In the rest of this book, more evidence is added to these main points.

Chapter 2.

What is Hell?

There are many explanations in the Bible and other religious books of the idea of hell. They are mostly places of punishment in ancient times which are usually used as a synonym for the 'destination of the wicked'. Just like the use of Calvary, in Christianity, as synonymous with the crucifixion of Christ.

However, I want to draw our attention to something that is scientifically possible. A hell that is so real, it is such a terrifying thought. The destruction of our solar system when the sun runs out of fuel.

Scientists have predicted that there are five thousand million years left before our sun runs out of energy. Our solar system has survived for 10 billion years and there are 5 billion years left. As the end approaches, the sun will begin to expand into a 'red giant' which will be 100 times or bigger than its current size. It will engulf the closest planets and probably melt them with the intense heat. This expansion into a red giant may take a long time, probably millions of years.

When the sun cannot expand or reaches its maximum expansion, it will collapse. The rate of collapse will determine its future. If it is greater than the speed of light, the sun will turn into a black hole because nothing will escape from it. All the planets of the solar system will be sucked into the black hole, the speed of collapse creates such a huge force, all the planets and everything will be crushed into nothing.

The alternative is not much better, if the rate of collapse is slower than the speed of light, the sun cools and becomes a stone planet known as a 'white dwarf' no bigger than the size of the earth. All the planets of the solar system are released from the sun's gravity, because the 'stone planet' is much smaller with less gravity. The planets will probably be thrown into space at the same speed they were revolving. They may spend some time burning up as they fly off or might crash into other objects in space. The gas planets like Jupiter might just explode and disappear. It will be gradual and may take millions of years, but Science has evidence to back up the destruction of our solar system from observing other stars going through that same process of expansion and death.

There is nothing more scary than being burned by the expanding sun. Suppose it is already happening? Is the sun beginning to expand and warms the earth? Is that the real reason for global warming? Are we going to be engulfed and melted into the eternal fire that is the sunshine? That is a hell fire that is more real than any other hell in history or the Bible.

Scientists have proved that even a small change in earth's temperature will be disastrous. Since 1880, earth's temperature has risen by 2°C, that is enough to drive what is known as global warming. Here's an excerpt from Climate.gov;

> Given the size and tremendous heat capacity of the global oceans, it takes a massive amount of heat energy to raise Earth's average yearly surface temperature even a small amount. The 2-degree increase in global average surface temperature that has occurred since the pre-industrial era (1880-1900) might seem small, but it means a significant increase in accumulated heat. That extra heat is driving regional and seasonal temperature extremes, reducing snow cover and sea ice, intensifying heavy rainfall, and changing habitat ranges for plants and animals—expanding some and shrinking others.

Imagine if the global temperature rise by 10°C or even just 5°C? There will be so much extreme weather on earth that human habitation might cease altogether! That is a hell that is so terrible, and so near, I prefer not to think about it.

What can we do about it? How can we save mankind from this approaching destruction?

It appears we already have the answers. If we can escape and return to God then we do not have to endure the painful and sinful earth anymore. We need to know more about this phenomenon. Can we produce Scientific proof of life after death? And of the destination of souls as they leave the Earth?

There are many scientific programmes all over the world studying the possibility of the existence of a soul. Many Scientists are convinced that the soul exists. Even artificial intelligence computers are being built that can replicate the human with a possible disastrous future called a 'singularity' when machines are more intelligent and capable than humans.

Humans might become slaves of their creation or worse, be exterminated by the machines.

Chapter 3.

The Ark of the Covenant

I was watching a Parable documentary on You Tube narrated by Meriam Henein, where a group of Americans tried to reconstruct the 'Ark of the Covenant' as described in the Christian Bible. Their theory was, in order for it to work like it did in the Bible stories, it has to store energy in it like a capacitor.

According to the Bible, Moses had the Ark of the Covenant built to hold the Ten Commandments, instructed by God. The Israelites carried the Ark with them during their 40 years spent wandering in the desert. It is said that when the Philistines conquered Israel and took the ark, they were afflicted with sores and so it was returned. Death would result if anyone looked inside it.

The proposal that the Ark is a capacitor suggest that it had stored a huge amount of energy which is somehow released on those daring to touch it, killing them, as related in the Bible.

A capacitor works when there is a source of energy causing accumulation of a positive and negative charge on the plates, separated by inert material. Potential energy is created. When a light bulb is introduced into the circuit and closed, the flow of electrons from the negative to the positive charge is indicated by the glow of the light bulb.

The Americans in the documentary suggest that the outside of the Ark, while it is being carried through the desert, with the cherubims and box covered in gold, would accumulate static and electromagnetic energy becoming negatively charged and the inside of the box, which is separated by the neutral wood, also covered in gold will be positively charged. The stored voltage of potential energy, would be big enough to kill anyone touching it.

They did build a replica of the ark according to biblical dimensions and tested the theory by lining the ark with copper plates, because gold would be too expensive, and applied electricity to it. The cherubims wings, which were metal, sparked and the whole thing burst into flames.

It does support the proposal is feasible, that static electrical and electromagnetic energy could have caused those events, when sparks zapped anyone touching the ark or coming near it.

Meriam, from the documentary, showed evidence from carvings or drawings on pyramid and ancient tomb walls that electrical gadgets and light bulbs may have been tested in ancient Egypt.

The ark was build to protect the stone tablets with the 10 commandments inside it according to biblical accounts. It seems that electrical technology was available or known during the time of Moses or earlier.

Whatever the 'capacitor technology' used to protect the stone tablets, it certainly is very advanced.

Near Death Experiences (NDE)

There are millions of reports suggesting that there is a soul which leaves the body during near death experiences in hospitals around the world. Reports of NDEs go back a long time.

There is even reports of reincarnated spirits that have come back in a different body in a different time and age. Many of them have been verified to be genuine thus giving support to the existence of the soul or spirit being. The current Dalai Lama of Tibet is one example of a reincarnation of a former Dalai Lama. The literature and stories support it, which is why he was chosen.

Many stories suggest that certain believers and practitioners of the soul and reincarnation camp go as far as suggesting that we are spirit beings having a human experience.

God is Energy

In my first 4 books called 'God is Energy. Do You Believe?', I had put forward the idea that, as explained in the trinity section of this book, God exists as omniscient and omnipotent intelligent energy and that God can manifest itself in various powerful ways.

We can also see from the trinity explanation that there is scientific support for the idea that God exist in a timeless universe where there is no beginning or end, just like a parallel universe proposed in modern science theory.

Is it possible then that God had accompanied the Israelites on their journey from Egypt to Canaan as a guardian housed in the covenant? Or is the covenant simply a 'battery' like modern electricity that bring God like power into play when required? Just like dead bodies are 'repowered' and revived by electrical currents in modern hospitals?

The Americans in the Meriam documentary suggest that the ark was just a trick to keep the Israelites following Moses, but that would mean that the whole of the Old Testament is just a series of fictional stories. And like any ancient Kingdom, many tricks and initiatives are used to keep the people under control. One example, is King Herod slaying or murdering all the children under 2 years old to prevent any challenge to his throne.

The fact that faith can move mountains according to Christ and modern records suggest that many modern Christian faithful had indeed performed miracles, does support the biblical narrative that God did indeed accompany the Israelites. The evidence does support it.

For example, the success of Jesus Christ and Christianity. The revival of the State of Israel. The establishment of the Kingdom of God on Earth as discussed already in this book and the God is Energy series. They are all evidence that God's plan as revealed in the Bible and its stories are being implemented. Our test for significance is satisfied. There is 100% correlation between the Bible stories and historical developments on earth. What else could cause it? It simply cannot happen by accident or randomly.

PART III

HOW CAN YOU TELL GOD'S INFLUENCE IN YOUR LIFE?

Chapter 1.

God's hand or random events?

In statistical inference, you can be confident that events happen for a reason if they test to be significant at 95% levels or higher. This is usually expressed as $P=0.05$. If the test is not significant then we conclude that it is just a natural occurrence.

But when you do not have a test you can compare the event with others of similar occurrences and see if it is a likely natural happening or not.

The events I related in Part I are just some things that happened in my life which are very likely to be 'caused by something' rather than it being a natural progression of human development. That is why I attribute them to God. God directs man to do his miracles as in many cases like Moses, Noah and the flood, Elijah, the 12 apostles and so on.

I would like to discuss some of the other 'strange occurrences' in my life which can only be attributed to the supernatural.

1. I heard the beast roar

I have related this account many times and I am getting more and more convinced that it was not entirely natural. When I started writing the first book of the 'God is Energy. Do you Believe?' series, my computer at home kept on breaking down so I went to the local library and continued on their computer, saving my work on a USB. At about 11.30 am I walked home and made a sandwich, getting ready to watch the 12pm news. Then the loudest clap of thunder shook our house as if by an earthquake. It lasted several seconds and I seem to hear the sound was like a beast roaring. It was very similar to the Beast in the movie 'Godzilla'. There was deathly quiet after and I noticed I am shaking a bit. That was the second time I feel that the 'beast' is displeased with what I am doing.

The other 2 times have been a 'snarl like' whisper as if somebody is warning me about something. I can definitely feel it's from a beast with a head as big as my room. I can just feel the power of it. I can make out that it was speaking, the kind of gibberish you only hear from aliens in movies like Star Wars, but from an animal as big as the one in Godzilla or bigger. I looked around but I cannot see anything, it was the same similar surroundings I am used to.

I am beginning to think that the 'beast' don't like what I am writing. I really think that God was pushing the beast away from me. That is why it roared so loudly. I have never heard it again for 2 years now.

Here's a poem I wrote that describe how I feel about that event.

Its called 'The Devil'.

THE DEVIL

The Bible say he is Lucifer

An angel of the stars

He was next only to God

But he thought he was the Lord

He disobeyed and vanished

He was forever banished

To become the evil one

He wanders the earth

And claim everyone since birth

He corrupt them with his evil ways

Til the end of their days

Then God became a man

To help humans understand

When their earthly body die

They can have everlasting life

His death and resurrection

Is the key to our salvation

When dust return to dust

He will claim our spirit he is just

And the Evil One will have to run

When God take over

He will have no fun

> Note: The reference to Lucifer as the Devil comes from Isaiah 14:12, in the King James Version 'How art thou fallen from heaven, O Lucifer, son of the morning, which didst weaken nations!'

I think this is how the evil one affects our lives, it corrupts us with wrong doing to displease God. To destroy our chances of ever returning to God.

We may ask. What's in it for the beast? How will the Devil benefit from our destruction?.

In my book called 'The Anti-Christ', I propose that the Devil or the Anti-Christ is the 'polar opposite' of God. John gives us a glimpse of this power in 1 John: 1-7

Beloved, believe not every spirit, but try the spirits whether they are of God: because many false prophets are gone out into the world. Hereby know ye the Spirit of God: Every spirit that confesseth that Jesus Christ is come in the flesh is of God: And every spirit that confesseth not that Jesus Christ is come in the flesh is not of God: and this is that spirit of antichrist, whereof ye have heard that it should come; and even now already is it in the world. **Ye are of God, little children, and have overcome them: because greater is he that is in you, than he that is in the world.** *They are of the world: therefore speak they of the world, and the world heareth them. We are of God: he that knoweth God heareth us; he that is not of God heareth not us. Hereby know we the spirit of truth, and the spirit of error. Beloved, let us love one another: for love is of God; and every one that loveth is born of God, and knoweth God*

John proposes that he that is in us, or the Holy Spirit, is stronger than he that is in the world. I believe he is referring to the evil one. The Devil, Satan, the one who will not acknowledge the coming of Jesus Christ. The Anti-Christ. The Polar Opposite of God. There are many such references to the Devil throughout the New Testament.

It is the Christian view that only Jesus Christ is the star in the Bible and the Devil is the 'polar opposite'. Everything that is good is found in Christ and everything that is bad is found in the Devil, the Beast, Satan, the Anti-Christ or whatever name it is called. When one is in Christ he/she becomes holy like Christ.

2. The Butterfly

In this story, I want to point to the arrival of the monarch butterfly during our song about a butterfly. We were just writing a song but what happened was really magical. I really believe that in life, this is how God touches us. It is the wonderful events and occurrences in our lives that show us the 'hand of God'.

I have also had experiences with other animals too. Dogs for example, sometimes give me the feeling that they are 'human', in the way they look straight into my eyes, wagging their tail and tongue as if they are so happy to see me.

In my garden, I am always greeted by two tiny fantails who flip around chirping as if they are happy to see me. But what happened with the butterfly gave me goosebumps. That is why I keep telling the story.

I was collecting feijoas with my 4 year old grandson because he loved eating feijoas after I gave him a plate full of it a few times. My intention was to give him a lot of vitamins because he had a skin condition that looks to me to be just a diet problem. I have been feeding the kid every morning from the abundance of ripe feijoas under our tree, which had fallen during the night. The kid was always up early, and knocked on my door, to wake me up for the morning routine of collecting feijoas from under the tree.

After we collected the fruits, we sit down with a knife and spoon and I cut them, scoop out the juicy, sweet flesh and give it to the kid. After he could eat no more, I ate the rest, then we sat down and he wanted to sing some songs.

We made up a song and it goes like this;

'Butterfly, butterfly come in here and hide. Hide from the storm, hide from the storm until its gone…

And the kid added this verse;

'Then you can go, you can go and find your Mum and Dad, And somewhere you belong'

Firstly, it really struck me as odd that the kid can come up with such a fitting verse. I had explained to him that the butterfly is imaginary and it is flying through a storm.

Then while we were singing, a large monarch butterfly came down and alighted on our orange tree about five meters from where we were sitting. It was a bright sunny morning with a clear blue sky. I saw the butterfly, its colours so bright in the sunshine, and the kid saw it too. He pointed and looked up at me laughing. It was only an average sized orange tree about 2-3 metres high.

It also struck me as strange that I rarely see any monarch butterflies around our house, but for it to turn up at that moment while we are singing is really amazing. It just fits in with what I was doing for the kid, the love I feel for him. I think that during that moment God touched us in a way that I will never forget. The butterfly denoting the beauty of love, my love for the kid and how amazing that moment was.

The 'growl of the monster' and the 'butterfly' events are just two of the occurrences which I believe gives me a feeling that there are spiritual powers around me which try to communicate. In other words, God touches us everyday but very often we miss the moment. We are too distracted with the world that we do not see the simple amazing happenings in our lives.

I can tell you some other stories but I don't think you will believe them. All I can say is that, when things keep happening that you cannot really explain, God is trying to show you something. Like my life in Part I, there is only one explanation for it. God's hand is touching me in ways that give me success where others fail.

The growl of the monster is a reminder that the 'Antichrist' is very real.

When I am struck down like Saul, on the road to Damascus, when I broke my collarbone in a rugby game; God is closing that door and opened a better path for me. A far greater path that raised me from mediocrity to a life of above average achievements which has not stopped since the famous evangelists opened my eyes to a gift that only God can provide.

If you look back in your lives, you will see certain patterns and things that have happened which changed your life forever. Many people have told me that it was Jesus Christ that changed their lives forever and I believe it. I have seen so many miracles in my life, it cannot be just random events.

3. The Birds Sing your Praises Lord

I wrote a song called 'Jesus Lord of My Life' and the last verse is about how God feeds the birds in his garden. Everywhere we see birds feeding on fruit trees and insects. They don't have to grow food or store them.

It is about Matthew 6:26;

Look at the birds of the air; they do not sow or reap or store away in barns, and yet your heavenly Father feeds them. Are you not much more valuable than they?

It is an amazing song because every time I sing it I feel much better after.

The last verse say;

> *'The birds sing your praises Lord*
> *As they feed in your garden*
> *And I sing your praises Lord*
> *The way you saved me'*

Many times I sung it at our old house and birds come and sing on our tree next to the house. I noticed they are especially active when I sing the song when I record it. I made some comments about it then forgot for a few years.

A few months later we moved to a new house. I sang and recorded the song after 2 years, at the new house, and guess what happened? When I came to the last verse a flock of birds arrived and started singing on the tree outside! I have it on record!

Is that simply coincidence?

Many people may doubt it, but it is happening too often. Like the butterfly, birds seem to turn up at the most uncanny times and sing on a tree outside!

I really believe that is how God interacts with man. God will speak to us through the environment and nature. The birds, the insects, the animals, the fish other humans. Sometimes God speaks directly to us through our 'inner self', he helps us make decisions, improve our lives and families. I have often wondered about the so called 'light bulb moments' when new discoveries are made. Is it God opening the door for us as Jesus promised?

Giving us the knowledge that we seek?. I really think so. It is important that we take the time to contemplate, meditate, pray and speak to God. It will fulfill our longing and emptiness and give us 'inner peace'.

4. A friend is gone

When I was doing my Master of Science at the University of Auckland, I was a member of the Squash Club and we played squash in various clubs during our season. One guy was a very regular beer drinking buddy after the games. We would have a few drinks and discuss topics of Philosophy, Christianity and Science.

One night while working late in the University laboratory, I had this very strong feeling that somebody had just entered the lab. I walked around and checked all the rooms but I was the only one there. It was close to 10 pm at night and I was feeling a bit scared. I used to be scared of ghosts as a kid, from all the ghost stories in Tongan villages.

I decided to go home, so I turned all the lights off and left.

Next morning I got off the bus and was walking down Symond Street, in the middle of campus, to the lab when I met my friend's son. We had some small talk then I asked about his Dad. How is he?. The kid started crying. He said his father passed away the previous night at about the same time I had that experience in the lab!

I have never had an experience with ghosts or spirits before but at that moment I was a believer. I offered the kid some condolences and gave him my number if he needs some help or moral support.

5. **Witches and Witch Craft**

In my research before writing this book, I would read books, watch documentaries and look up records of certain points I want to make on Google and other search engines. I was interested in what other writers have to say about my views. In the search for what others think of my experiences I came across some really shocking views.

In Europe, especially in England and Greater Britain, witches have been practicing their dark art for centuries. It was illegal in the past but have somehow gained some legal support and even followings. It is totally legal and even fashionable to be a witch in modern Europe and Britain these days.

Witches even claim a lot of miracles as part of their repertoire of magic. On one occasion, one very normal elderly woman in rural England wanted to know why she is having a lot of unexplained 'miracles' in her life and she was told by the local Witches Association that she must be a witch or was a witch in the past.

I had explained in the God is Energy series why I think black magic works, just the same with Christian prayers, but it was a really shocking revelation that my theory was verified in that way.

6. God and Man

The fact that witches can claim to perform magic just like Christians pray and believe God will grant their wishes, point to an interesting phenomenon. Many records suggest that miracles do happen in non-Christian circles, in fact the Bible does point out that the Devil is perfectly capable of performing miracles.

Just like in the story of Moses, when he threw his staff on the floor it turned into a snake, but so did Pharaoh's magicians! They were able to replicate God's power, but then the 'snake of Moses' ate all the other snakes - which is a very important point to remember. Even though the Devil may exhibit power like Jesus Christ, the power of Christ can overcome the Devil as supported by 1 John 4:4.

It does bring us back to the point already discussed, of John's view about the Anti-Christ. The 'one inside us' is stronger than the 'one out there'.

But our test for significance here is the ability of man to perform miracles, which proves our theory that there is something causing it. Something or someone is causing these miracles to happen. Christians believe it to be God while the 'other corner' believe it to be the Anti-Christ.

However, as already pointed out God's power will overcome that of the Devil.

Chapter 2.

Is your life full of riches but still feels empty?

I have heard so many people talk about it, they work so hard to get a house, get a nice car, get all the comfort they want, but after getting all of it, it still feels empty. There was a missing ingredient in their lives. Then they found Jesus Christ and now they feel fulfilled.

It is a bit like the dead body being raised using an electric current at the hospital. The body has all the parts intact but it is still dead, only when energy is applied to it that it becomes alive again. The missing ingredient was the energy to give it life.

In nature, there are some animals that spent their life in one place but when its time to breed they migrate a long way to another place where they all meet with the other members of the species. Some birds, whales, salmon are just some of these migratory animals. The animals know where they are going. They have never been there before, because after they breed they die. Only the large animals like whales breed and keep returning. Salmon, for example, will die after breeding and their bodies become a fresh load of food for the river ecosystem where they breed and decompose. In most cases we have seen in documentaries, the Salmon are born in the rivers and then migrate to live in the sea, returning only to breed and die.

How do the animals know where to go? It seems they already know where they are going when they start off, even if its a thousand miles away. Something in their bodies has recorded that message or knowledge and pass it on like a genetic code.

That is like man.

We always know that we need God in our lives. We can feel that there is something missing, we feel unfulfilled despite the earthly riches of our lives.

Like the spirits that know the body needs it to live, the body also knows that it needs the spirit to become fulfilled. There is only one spirit in the universe. God.

I have felt it myself many times, that I am feeling unworthy and unfulfilled. But I do remember that when I quietly contemplate the infinite. When I think about God and creation. When I sing my gospel songs. When I pray and read the Bible. I can feel the emptiness disappearing and the Holy Spirit taking over. I can feel the power of God in my life. I can feel the energy.

I keep saying this in many of my writings. It is so obvious that most people never give it a second thought, but read the Lord's prayer and think about it.

This is what Jesus Christ taught his disciples to say when they pray;

The Lord's Prayer

Our Father which art in heaven

Hallowed be thy name

Thy Kingdom come.

Thy will be done on Earth as it is in heaven.

Give us this day our daily bread and forgive us our

trespasses, as we forgive them that trespass against us.

Lead us not into temptation and deliver us from evil.

For thine is the Kingdom the Power and the Glory.

For ever and ever. Amen.

If you think about it carefully, everything that the Lord's prayer talks about has happened in the past 2,000 years. Note the words 'Thy Kingdom come', you can be sure that this already happened. The Catholic Church which was called the Universal Church when it began in the first century is a Sovereign State with the Pope as its Monarch or Head of State.

According to Wikipedia, Vatican city became the Vatican State, and independent from Italy, with the Lateran Treaty in 1929. It is a distinct territory under 'full ownership, exclusive dominion and sovereign authority and jurisdiction of the Holy See'. A sovereign entity under international law which maintains the city states temporal, diplomatic and spiritual independence.

It has an area of 49 hectares or 121 acres with a population of 805 making it the smallest sovereign state in the world by area and population. However, it is headquarters to the biggest church in Christianity. The Catholic Church known as the Universal Church in ancient times. It is the Kingdom of God or Holy See.

At the end the Lord's prayer confirms it.

'For thine is the Kingdom, the Power and the Glory'.

The Catholic Church is the biggest Christian Organisation in the World. It is the biggest charity in the world. It is also the biggest church in the world. Together with the other Christian Groups, they dominate everything on earth. You can have no doubts as to who has the power and the glory on earth. God.

The second biggest religion on Earth, with 1.8 billion members according to the latest statistics, also worship God, Islam.

It does raise another question. If God is giving us our daily bread, forgive us our sins and protect us from evil, we are basically well looked after! Every dollar you make was made in a Christian community with the passion of Christ to help the needy. Every charity in the world that help poor communities and countries are Christian in faith. Every miracle on earth was inspired by none other than, you guessed it, Christ himself.

So why are we feeling unfulfilled in a community of plenty?

There is only one answer. The Devil is keeping us blind to God's designs and gifts for our lives. Like in the poems wording, when you let God take over, the Devil will have to 'run away'. He will growl and disapprove but he cannot fight God. God is too powerful as the apostle John points out 'the one inside us is stronger'.

Try it. Let God become your savior and guide. All you have to do is ask in prayer.

Try the Lord's prayer or even think about it quietly. Repeating it often during the day, everyday in your mind. It will quickly bring you peace.

Do you feel life is not worth living?

There are many young people who feel that life is no longer worth living. In New Zealand, according to the Ministry of Health, there were 654 people who died from suicide, the previous year to June 2020.

Statistics show that the age group 15-24 have the highest numbers of death from suicide with Maori youth as the most affected followed by Pacific Islanders. There seem to be a correlation between suicide and the most deprived areas. It does seem that poverty is the most likely cause of suicides in New Zealand.

To day I saw a video by Andrew Fifita, the famous and very successful Australian rugby league player of Tongan origin, about his apparent suicide attempt. It did seem he was affected by alcohol but he normally does not drink.

Many other well known and successful rugby league young players have attempted suicide.

The wealthy and famous of Hollywood apparently suffer from the same depression and self loathing. More than 40 stars, the most famous of whom is household name and comedian, Robin Williams, committed suicide. It seems fame, wealth and even beauty is not enough.

It seems that in New Zealand, deprivation is the cause of suicide but in Hollywood, success or the apparent trappings of success also cause suicide, or maybe a failing career. But if you have accumulated enough to live on for several lifetimes why do you need to be the centre of attention and success?

Why do people commit suicide?

It seems from the teachings of all the famous prophets and philosophies of every major religion, there is one problem.

Man's sole existence on earth is to try and achieve nirvana, moksha or holiness so he or she can return to God. It logically follows therefore, that one must purposely and with love and dedication seek God. The absence of God from one's life is the problem. In my book, 'The Antichrist' I have attempt to explain why.

It seems that the 'one out there' as pointed out by the apostle John, has great power and can lure the unwitting to its camp.

As I say in the poem 'The Devil', he 'claims everyone since birth and corrupt them with his evil ways'.

We are all weak humans, we do not have the power to beat the devil on our own. That is why we need Jesus Christ, God on our side. As the apostle pointed out 'the one inside you is stronger'.

I would challenge everyone who feels depression to say the Lord's prayer 100 times everyday and meditate, read the bible and sing some hymns everyday.

Jesus Christ has promised that if you ask, you shall receive. The Holy Spirit will come and fill your existence with love and power. The Devil will have no choice but to leave.

There is no doubt that people who have found Christ and follow his teachings are saved. Make Christ your savior by saying his prayer 100 times a day, meditate and read the bible everyday.

I watch a lot of You Tube videos about topics I am researching and it is very useful for my writing, but more importantly, my life as a Christian.

You don't have to be religious or attend church every day. Just set aside some time to meditate on Christ and his teachings, read the Bible and think about the meaning of life and death.

000

PART IV

THE FIVE PILLARS OF CHRIST

Chapter 1.

Faith

As Christians, it is important that we have an active relationship with God, whether we are active in church or not. The historical influence of Christianity on Western Society can be seen in our Laws, Regulations and Social Etiquette. Most Western Societies practice the pillars of Christ especially love, hope and charity, even though they do not attend Church.

Jesus did say that we do not just pray in Jerusalem or the temple we pray everywhere and anyone can pray to God. Not just the Jews.

In John 4: 21-24, Jesus declared to the Sumerian woman;

> *"Woman," Jesus replied, "believe me, a time is coming when you will worship the Father neither on this mountain nor in Jerusalem. You Samaritans worship what you do not know; we worship what we do know, for salvation is from the Jews. Yet a time is coming and has now come when the true worshipers will worship the Father in the Spirit and in truth, for they are the kind of worshipers the Father seeks. God is spirit, and his worshipers must worship in the Spirit and in truth."*

Christianity arose from the Jews. Jesus Christ was born a Jew, but there is also the biblical old Testament to consider in the totality of Christian understanding. Since creation and the books of Moses, the story of the Israelites and their sufferings are the inspiration for Christianity.

Its important to note, that in John 4 verses 23 and 24, Jesus allows everyone to worship God but they must worship in spirit and in truth. In other words, spirit and truth are key elements of faith. Jesus predicted that a time will come when everyone, not only the Jews, will worship God.

This may be the reason why Jesus chose and converted St Paul, because St Paul preached the gospel to Jews and non-Jews. It was St Paul's influence that brought Christianity to the whole world. There is no doubt that Jesus Christ chose Saul for that reason. To bring his message to the gentiles. The non-Jews.

An example of faith, the ministry of St Paul

St Paul was also a citizen of Rome, which allows him certain privileges. He was a well trained and highly educated Jew. The other followers of Christ led by James, brother of Jesus, preferred to stick with the Jewish approach to Christianity, only allowing Jews into their group.

There were many disagreements between Paul and James. Paul was preaching to Jews and non-Jews. There were many Jewish laws that were not acceptable to non-Jews, like circumcision which became a huge problem for Paul. He was travelling around the nearby regions establishing churches but James and his group preferred to stay in Jerusalem and preach only to Jews. James finally summoned Paul and demanded that he observe Jewish law and be cleansed and purified in the temple. But the Jews had other ideas, Paul was almost killed by a mob and was only saved by his Roman citizenship, the Roman guards taking him away.

The key here is Paul's 'preaching to non-Jews'. In some references Paul mentioned that it is the 'risen Jesus' who had called him to his service. He did not seem to want anything to do with the historical Jesus of Nazareth or was probably affected by Jewish tradition.

Paul's faith was in the death and resurrection of Christ, which is the power of God incarnate, not the 'genealogy or historical Jesus' as some writers put it. The genealogy and historical Jesus also has a problem with the Jewish leaders who do not believe what Jesus was saying.

There is a very, very important aspect of Paul's ministry. Most of the denial of Christianity today has to do with the historical Jesus. Was there a man called Jesus Christ? His very existence is in question let alone his divine origin. It was Paul's epistles, his letters to the churches. The 13 books in the Bible's New Testament that gives Jesus Christ concrete and irrevocable proof. It is almost a literary resurrection of the historical Jesus. In it we can see the hand of God. The very reason why Paul was chosen. All the other books in the Bible's New Testament were written by others, like the 4 gospels but attributed to Matthew,

Mark, Luke and John. They were probably 'ghost writers' as they call them today, taking dictation from the apostles or their followers.

It is noted that certain writers think the book of Hebrews was not written by St Paul, otherwise it would be 14 books under St Paul's authorship.

It is also worth mentioning that it was Paul's ministry that established the Christian movement, globally, James and his group in Jerusalem were absorbed back into the Jewish mainstream. There are some records suggesting they became a secretive sect but little is known about them.

Obviously, it was the faith of the gentiles that saved the Christian faith not only from being wiped out by the Romans but also dying out completely under Jewish persecution.

Both Rome and the Jewish nation vanished as predicted by Jesus Christ.

What is most amazing, as we now realize, that the Jews themselves would have been wiped out. It was the Christians who saved the Jews from certain extinction. Firstly, by saving the Jews from worldwide persecution as the 'killers of Christ' and also giving the Jews a homeland in the Holy land where they have been removed for more than 1,000 years under the sword of Islam. In 1948, the Christian countries of the United Nations supported the creation of Israel which has been under British protection and management since 1929.

> It is an interesting aside that both Israel and the Vatican were recognised as 'nations' in 1929. Was it a master stroke of man or divine direction? The Vatican became a sovereign state in 1929 and Israel was later established in 1948.

The Moslems still refuse to recognize Israel as a nation. There are 30 Moslem nations, for example, who do not recognize Israel as a nation. It is only the protection of the Christians that keep Israel in existence. For example, the United States of America.

It is an interesting fact, Israel's main religion is Judaism which does not recognize Jesus Christ as the son of God yet Jesus Christ is their main protector. Christians believe Jesus Christ to be the son of God or what the Hindus would say an 'avatar of God'. Jesus Christ is also one of the prophets of Islam. That is probably why Islam does not support the State of Israel and would prefer it to be destroyed.

Faith in Christianity

Faith is very, very important in Christianity. Without faith a Christian will find it difficult to practice his convictions as a follower of Jesus Christ.

In Hebrews 11: 1-40, faith is explained.

'Now faith is being sure of what we hope for and certain of what we do not see'.

Abel, Enoch, Noah, Abraham, Isaac, Jacob, Moses and many others are given as examples of the faithful.

There is one important point. The faithful trust in God's integrity and his word, it has not failed them in the past and will not fail in the future. There is one important difference between the Christian faith and all other religions. The death and resurrection of Jesus Christ, son of God. God the Son. As noted in the section explaining the trinity, God is the Son in the flesh and blood, a manifestation of the word.

'The heavens and the earth will pass away but my words will not pass away'

Matthew 24:35

It is a very strong link to;

'In the beginning was the Word, and the Word was with God, and the Word was God.

John 1:1

Note that in the gospels, the words of Jesus Christ has power to heal. In many of the miracles, all Christ has to do was *'say the word and they were healed'* as *revealed in the faith of the Centurion.* Matthew 8:8.

Faith as religion

St Paul talks about the resurrection of the body as very important to clearly separate Christianity from all other faiths. The resurrection proves the divinity of Christ, an imagery of God's triumph over death. Paul's 2 years under house arrest in Rome is probably the most important in terms of influencing the Romans and spreading the Christian faith. He was still preaching the gospel while under restrictions.

It is very, very important to emphasize that without St Paul, Christianity may have never existed! That is proof that divine intervention and selection of St Paul by Jesus Christ had direction and psychic foresight.

Some Christians called Agnostics suggest that the story of Christ was more like an allegory. That the deeper meanings and teachings of Christianity is the more important part of the story of Jesus. However, as we shall see later and developed in this argument, that there is evidence of the existence of the historical Jesus without which 'the risen Jesus' could not exist in history. That is a very important point if the Christian faith.

We shall also discuss how the existence of the soul, with scientific proof, adds much credibility to the Christian faith.

A scientific approach to faith

There is an important note from my discussion of the Trinity and how Albert Einstein's Theory of Relativity helps us understand God. While St Paul's faith is based on the resurrection and Jesus appearing to more than 500 people, that his physical body has risen from the dead, the theory of relativity gives us a scientific basis for such an occurrence.

The theory of relativity gives us the scientific explanation of how mass and energy are interchangeable under the right conditions. It does give credibility to the resurrection of Christ because it is entirely possible in the realm of science for a body to exist in mass or energy form, both being equal and the same object!

In our example of water existing in 3 states like God, we can see that only one state can exist at any one time. If we can only see ice, we know that it can also be liquid or steam. Faith is saying that we believe in the existence of the 3 states of water. We cannot claim that water as steam or liquid does not exist just because we can only see ice.

Like wise, we cannot claim that God the Father and God the Holy Spirit do not exist because we can only see, and touch, God the Son.

It should be pointed out, the death and resurrection of Jesus Christ, as God the Son is just a demonstration by God that the saving grace of man is God itself.

There is also a fourth dimension to our water example, water also evaporate and form clouds up above. Then fall as rain, under the right conditions, thus giving life to the earth. Life cannot exist without water.

Similarly, man cannot exist without God, just like life on earth cannot exist without water.

Faith in God's grace

St Paul mentions grace in all his epistles. He emphasizes to his fellow Christians in the churches he helped to build that God's grace is the most important divine blessing for the faithful. Grace, as used in Christianity, is defined by most literature as;

'unmerited favor of God towards man'

I have discussed the letter of Paul to the Ephesians 2:8, in book 3 of the 'God is Energy. Do you Believe?' series, which is a key to our understanding;

'For it is by grace that you have been saved. It is not from yourselves. It is a gift from God'

> **An example of faith from St James 1:5**
>
> *If any of you lacks wisdom, you should ask God, who gives generously to all without finding fault, and it will be given to you. But when you ask, you must believe and not doubt, because the one who doubts is like a wave of the sea, blown and tossed by the wind.*

Faith in the resurrection of Christ

While St Paul emphasizes the death and resurrection of Christ as key and cornerstone to the Christian faith and salvation, we should not forget that God is capable of anything. God is omniscient and omnipotent. That is the key to the power of the Trinity. The manifestations of God.

St Paul was preaching at a time when there were other forces against him. First, the Roman Empire and secondly the Jewish leadership. The Romans put him in jail and the Jewish leadership kills and maims his followers.

King Herod, for example, tried to kill Jesus by having all children, under 2 years old, killed to eliminate any possibility of challenges to his role as King, when rumors of a new King being born was the local gossip. Joseph and Mary were warned by an angel that they should escape to Egypt to avoid the child Jesus Christ being killed by King Herod and his soldiers. We can definitely see the hand of God at play there.

The Jewish leadership were later responsible for the crucifixion of Christ at the age of 30. We ask the question. Did God enable the crucifixion of Christ to allow for the resurrection and conversion of the human race? Wasn't it God's design all along?

Clearly the time of Christ and his disciples was a time of conflicting interests between the Roman Empire and the Jewish leadership. Not only in terms of political gain but philosophical and religious dogma.

It was a time of cruel and unbelievable hatred.

The fact that Jesus Christ arrived at this time is probably a 'divine intervention'. And I need to reiterate the point that 'although Judaism does not recognize Jesus Christ as the son of God, Jesus Christ is the protector of Judaism and the Jews'. Without Jesus Christ, the State of Israel will never be resurrected. It will still be under the sword of Islam.

Did God use the Romans and Islam to punish the Jews as Jesus predicted?

There is also one very important point here. Jesus Christ is called the 'Prince of Peace' and we now know peace to be the most sought after and valued state of the human society, especially in the Middle East and the State of Israel.

Jesus did say that he has come, but they did not recognize him.

One very important point about the teachings of Christ, at a time of hatred and cruelty, is that with faith comes love.

Faith in modern times

Imagine your local church Minister or Pastor being persecuted or jailed by government soldiers for preaching the gospel in 2020! That will be front page news all over the world in every newspaper and television channel. Every Christian all over the world will be up in arms!

We are living in a time of advanced technology and philosophy but as Christians we believe that all of that development are due to the intervention of Christ and the Holy Spirit.

I have already discussed in the 'God is Energy. Do You Believe? Series of books how the miracles of Christ reflects advanced scientific technology in this modern age. For example, the changing of water into wine can simply be a matter of adding alcohol and flavors and its done in a few minutes! But in the days of Christ they did not know that alcohol can be produced separately from the wine! And that flavors can give the wine many tastes foreign to their palettes. The miracle of raising the dead is performed daily in hospitals throughout the world by using electrical currents. Man has reproduced all of the miracles of Christ and millions of others.

How is that possible?

It seems that Christ had advanced knowledge that is 2,000 years in the future. All his miracles suggest that. But also he left and send the Holy Spirit to be man's helper for all of eternity. He told us 'Seek and you shall find, knock and the door shall be opened'. Science seeks all sorts of complicated answers to their scientific problems and they usually come up with a bright idea of solving it. The so called 'light bulb' moments.

Here's a good one I like to quote. Inventor Thomas Edison was said to have tried 5,000 times before he got the filament light bulb to work. The same effort have been quoted as 10,000 and 1,000 in some publications. Whatever the truth, it does emphasize the great effort put into the discovery and support the words of Christ.

'Seek and ye shall find. Knock and the door shall be opened.'

Who do you think gives man those 'light bulb' moments? Moments of inspiration that caused Archimedes to run naked along the road shouting 'eureka'. He has found it. The solution to his scientific problem.

Our faith is not in vain as St Paul suggested. We have the Holy Spirit. The Holy Spirit is man's helper and guide sent by Jesus Christ 2,000 years ago. The most powerful force in the world and dare I say it, the universe.

Would you say that the electricity is a miracle? If you turned on a filament light bulb to light up the room where the disciples meet, during the first century, would they consider it a miracle?

Of course they would. Even today, I still look at the light bulb and wonder. If energy causes the electron to flow and light up the filament, surely that light comes from God?

We may not believe in the existence of the electron, but the light bulb is proof of it. Similarly, in faith the Christians and their 'good work' on earth is proof that God and Jesus Christ exist.

So when Jesus said he is the light of the world, it was not just literal it was the fact! We can see how it connects with Einstein's theory where energy and matter are equal and the same.

But also faith breeds love and with love we can conquer anything.

Faith in the Holy Spirit

The Holy Spirit carries out the work Jesus had laid out for man. Here are some examples;

1. The Holy Spirit destroyed the Roman Empire and replaced it with God's Kingdom, the Bishop of Rome or the Pope as we know him is the Monarch of the Kingdom of God. A sovereign state known as the Holy See or Vatican.

The Roman Empire was the biggest army and most powerful in the world of Christ's time. But it was no match against the Holy Spirit. The spears and swords do not have any power against *'fire that arrives from heaven and sounds like a great wind'*, as the apostles describe the arrival of the Holy Spirit.

The Pope is the head of the biggest charity, church and Christian organization on Earth. Didn't Jesus say it to St Peter the first Pope?

'Upon this rock I shall build my church'.

Here is what Jesus said to Simon son of Jonah in Matthew 16:17-19.

Jesus replied, "Blessed are you, Simon son of Jonah, for this was not revealed to you by flesh and blood, but by my Father in heaven. And I tell you that you are Peter, and on this rock I will build my church, and the gates of Hades will not overcome it. I will give you the keys of the kingdom of heaven; whatever you bind on earth will be bound in heaven, and whatever you loose on earth will be loosed in heaven."

This is the passage that gives us a clue to Simon's appointment. Just like the appointment of Saul, who became Paul, on the road to Damascus. Simon was appointed the first Pope and he became Peter. We can tell from the power of the Holy See and the

Christians of to-day how important the appointment of St Paul and St Peter were to the development of Christianity in the whole world.

> An interesting note here is Saul of Tarsus was a Hebrew name, but Paul is actually a Roman equivalent! Peter is a Greek name and Simon (Shimon) is the Hebrew equivalent.

2. The Holy Spirit destroyed the Jewish leadership and replaced them with Islam. Islam and its armies occupied the Holy Land for more than 1,000 years. It was only the intervention of the Christians that resurrected the State of Israel in 1948. The followers of Jesus Christ decided to give the Jews a home but also to protect the Holy sites of the Christians. It was a gesture of charity worthy of Christ himself.

History accounts tells of a really amazing story. Firstly, the Christians, who have been persecuted for 3 centuries, won the Roman Empire over in the 4th Century but the fall of Rome and rise of Islam, in the 6th century, saw the Holy Land occupied by Islam for more than a 1,000 years until the British took over after World War I. It is very fortunate for the Jews that a Christian country had managed their affairs which finally culminated in the establishment of the State of Israel in 1948, after World War II. The domination of Christianity worldwide was the vehicle for Israeli Statehood and also freedom. The citizens of Israel to-day enjoys freedom just like any other free country. There are Christians, Moslem and other religions beside the majority Judaism religion, which is the 10th largest in the world with between 15-18 million adherents.

It is a very important point to make here, the claim by St Peter that Jesus Christ is the messiah is being fulfilled. Isn't it not the Christians or followers of Christ who gave the Jews a homeland? The British mandate given it by the league of nations, is official. It is stated in the records that the British had the desire to give the Jews a homeland. George VI was the King of the United Kingdom and Dominions and also Head of the Church of England.

Would you say, it is the hand of God? That delivered the land of Israel to the Jews with the army and blessing of King George VI, a Christian King?

It does remind us that many of the Christian Kings of Europe and Great Britain had been fighting to free

Jerusalem from Islam for 200 years before they gave up in the 13th century when the armies of Islam overran it.

The United States also played a very important role in supporting the fledgling Israelis by providing military defense until it was strong enough to defend itself. Since its formal recognition, in May 1948, to this day, some 72 years.

The international recognition of Israel refers to the diplomatic recognition of the State of Israel, which was established by the Israeli Declaration of Independence on 14 May 1948. Israel's sovereignty is disputed by some 30 Islamic countries because Israel does not recognize Jesus Christ as a prophet of Islam.

As of August 2020, 163 of the 193 UN member states recognize Israel.

Faith in the words of Christ

The words of Christ is discussed throughout this book, but lets look closely, in this section, at his predictions of the fall of the Jewish State and Roman Empire.

Jesus had predicted both the fall and destruction of the temple, which was a veiled reference to the coming destruction of the Jewish State and the Roman Empire supporting it.

In Matthew 24: 1-2;

'And Jesus went out from the temple, and was going on his way; and his disciples came to him to show him the buildings of the temple. But he answered and said unto them, 'You see all these things. Do you not? Truly I say unto you, there shall not be left here one stone upon another, that shall not be thrown down'.

And it did happen as we have discussed under the section on Titus Flavius Caesar, Emperor of Rome. In the year 70 CE, just 37 years from the crucifixion of Jesus, the Roman Army destroyed Jerusalem and most of Judea, only the 'desert was left'.

Titus Flavius Caesar did attribute the destruction of Israel to 'divine wrath' rather than the Roman Army! He is said to have 'refused a wreath' because of that belief. The arch celebrating his victory still stands in Rome to this day.

It is a very interesting and historical phenomenon that all of the prophecies of Christ occurred. All his words had an uncanny way of happening. The Jewish records claimed that Jesus practiced sorcery, but as we continue to analyze history according to the words and prophesies of Jesus Christ, there is no doubt at all that he was more than just a preacher. It all happened according to his words. It seems that Jesus Christ also has control of the future!

The fact that he chose St Paul to spread the gospel suggest he knew that only through the ministry of St Paul Christianity will survive.

It does remind us of what Jesus said in Matthew 24:35;

'Heaven and Earth shall pass away but my words will never pass away'

The fact that the Jewish records agreed there was a man called Jesus of Nazareth supports our claim, in Part V, that the historical Jesus did exist. But, of course, the Jewish records deny that Jesus was the messiah or son of God. They suggest that he may have been a preacher, preaching against the Roman occupation and he was crucified for it.

To-day we know that Jesus was much more than just a priest, all the evidence support it.

In Matthew 21:18-22

Now in the morning as he returned into the city, he hungered. And when he saw a fig tree in the way, he came to it, and found nothing thereon, but leaves only, and said unto it, Let no fruit grow on thee henceforward for ever. And presently the fig tree withered away. And when the disciples saw it, they marveled, saying, How soon is the fig tree withered'.

This is one prophecy in this analysis from Google, 'The cursing of the fig tree is an incident in the gospels, presented in Mark and Matthew as a miracle in connection with the entry into Jerusalem, and in Luke as a parable. The image is taken from the Old Testament symbol of the fig tree representing Israel, and the cursing of the fig tree in Mark and Matthew and the parallel story in Luke are thus symbolically directed against the Jews, who have not accepted Jesus as king'.

Can we take this explanation as another veiled prophecy of what was coming to the Jewish Kingdom? The destruction that will follow?

The Roman Empire and King Herod were ruling Judea together, during the time of Jesus and can be said to be both leaders of the Jewish State. It is very likely that the fate of both the Romans and Jewish State were intertwined in the prophesies and both as we shall see in the history accounts, both perished.

In the discussion of the Trinity, we can deduce from science that as explained in Einstein's equation of $E = mc^2$ that when the velocity approaches the velocity of light time stops. Time becomes irrelevant. In other words, in God's realm there is no time. No beginning or end. This is a very clear explanation of what is written in the book of Genesis reiterated in John 1:1.

'In the beginning was the Word, and the Word was with God, and the Word was God.'

What does that say about Jesus Christ? All the evidence so far support St Peter's claim, in Matthew 16:13-20 and Mark 8: 27-30, that *'Jesus Christ is the messiah, son of the living God.'*

It is supported by the fact that Jesus Christ is the savior and protector of modern Israel!

Faith in the work of the Holy Spirit

> **Faith with Deeds from St James**
>
> *What good is it, my brothers and sisters, if someone claims to have faith but has no deeds? Can such faith save them? Suppose a brother or a sister is without clothes and daily food. If one of you says to them, "Go in peace; keep warm and well fed," but does nothing about their physical needs, what good is it? In the same way, faith by itself, if it is not accompanied by action, is dead.*

Lastly, we would like to know how the Holy Spirit works. In these events we can see how God uses the Holy Spirit to effect the changes in the world.

1. The crucifixion and resurrection of Christ
2. The conversion of Paul
3. The sending of the Holy Spirit to the disciples
4. Paul preaching to non-Jews and getting a good following
5. Paul escaping to Rome
6. The appointment of Simon as the leader of the church
7. Destruction of Jerusalem and the Temple
8. Conversion of many Romans to Christianity

9. The conversion of Emperor Constantine
10. Christianity spreading to all corners of the known world

If we look a bit closer at all the events happening after the crucifixion, we can see the hand of God in everything. I have no doubt it is the work of the Holy Spirit after its arrival on Pentecost.

If we look at events during the last 2,000 years, we can see the hand of God in everything.

If you look at the events of today, you can see the hand of God in everything.

What does that tell you?

Like the light provided by the shining light bulb, is proof of the existence of the electron, so the events of the past 2,000 years as predicted by Christ and the biblical stories is proof of the existence of God.

Why?

Because we can see the effect of faith in Christ working miracles in the lives of Christians and shaping the history of mankind, just as we can see the light of the light bulb.

CHAPTER 2.

HOPE

Hope is a familiar word, unlike faith which is mostly to do with religious salvation, is applied in almost all walks of life. Hope is associated with every human endeavour that requires success as a way forward.

But what is hope in the Biblical sense? This is what the apostle Paul has to say.

Hope according to St Paul

St Paul had revealed that all his writings were revelations of Christ himself and it was God calling him to his service to preach to the Gentiles.

This is probably the most important and key revelation by Paul, the 13 or 14 books he wrote, which are included in the Christian Bible's New

Testament were written by Christ himself through him.

This is a very, very important phenomenon in Christianity. Just as Jesus Christ was an 'avatar' of God, so were the teachings the disciples taught their followers were revelations from Christ himself. We can tell the words coming out of the apostles is divine in nature.

I use the word avatar to add more evidence to the existence of Jesus Christ as God the Son, because the same idea also occur in other older religions like Hinduism. We say older because of historical records, but what can be older than God? For although Hinduism is 'historically older', God the Son, exist in a timeless parallel universe as explained in the Trinity Chapter where there is no beginning or end.

Note what St Paul is saying,

Galatians 1: 11-12

'For I would have you know, brothers, that the gospel that was preached by me is not man's gospel. For I did not receive it from any man, nor was I taught it, but I received it through a revelation of Jesus Christ.'

This is Paul's biggest statement on hope. He is informing the Galatian church that his writings and what he preaches is not from anyone, but Christ himself. Clearly, Paul wants to impress on the Galatians that although he had prosecuted the Christians mercilessly, Christ has called him to preach to the Gentiles.

Paul was beginning to have problems with the Jewish Christian Community who resent the fact that he is bringing Gentiles into the Church as well as the Temple.

In Galatians 1: 22-23, Paul is known as the man who tried to destroy the faith.

' I was personally unknown to the churches of Judea that are in Christ. They only heard the report: "The man who formerly persecuted us is now preaching the faith he once tried to destroy.'

Paul comes across as being vulnerable. In his vulnerability we can see his shining faith and hope in Christ. Especially the hope. It also comes across very clearly and with much strength that Paul takes pride in his work and is strengthened by his calling to do the bidding of his Lord Jesus Christ. That is the greatest incentive that gives him hope. That is the hope that Christians thrive on, that in Jesus Christ they will find salvation.

Hoping for what we do not have

The biblical definition of hope is confident expectation. Hope is a firm assurance regarding things that are unclear and unknown, through faith we can have hope. Paul was talking about hope for what is to come. That they should wait for it patiently. The glory that is theirs through redemption in Christ.

In Romans 8: 24-25, in Paul's letter he says;

'For in this hope we were saved. But hope that is seen is no hope at all. Who hopes for what he already has? But if we hope for what we do not have, we wait for it patiently.'

Paul, when he was still Saul, was an educated man, a Roman citizen, who despised the Christians and wanted to destroy them. He did not do it himself on his own accord, he got official approval from the High Priests of the Temple to arrest and put the Christians in chains. Paul was almost 30 years old at the time a few years after the crucifixion of Christ. It would have been the year 36 C.E. (Christian Era)*, that he was struck down and converted by Christ.

> * - it is the view of the author that Christian Era is more appropriate than Common Era.

It is an interesting aside that Saul, who persecuted the Christians, was a Jew. Saul of Tarsus was a Jewish name. But Paul is a Latin or Roman name. Was it because he was preaching to the Gentiles or was he hiding the fact that he used to persecute the Christians as Saul of Tarsus?

Paul's letter to the Romans, widely regarded as his masterpiece in terms of spiritual and redemption content, is also the longest of his epistles was written about 54 C.E. After 54, Paul began having problems with the Jewish Christians which culminated in his removal to Rome, for appealing to Caesar. But Caesar - Emperor Nero sentenced him to death by decapitation.

He was under house arrest for 2 years from 60-62 CE before his demise and he preached to the Romans gaining many converts during that period.

The prophesies of hope

There are recurring events in the history of early Christianity which are synonymous with the prophesies of Christ. Events that suggest divine intervention to punish the persecutors and destroyers of innocent Christians.

It gives hope to all Christians that God will punish those who do them wrong.

Here are some examples;

1. Emperor Nero had St Paul killed by decapitation

After St Paul's martyrdom in 62 CE several major events happened.

1. Rome was burned in 64 CE for 9 days. When the fire was eventually put out, 10 of Romes 14 districts were in ruins. It is said 66 per cent of Rome was destroyed.
2. The Jews rebelled in Judea, in 66 CE, killing all the Romans with both Kind Herod Agrippa II and the Roman Officials fleeing for their lives. That was the 12 year of Nero's reign.

3. Nero was ousted as Emperor in 68 CE, he committed suicide after being tried in absentia, by the Roman Senate and sentenced to death as 'public enemy'. He was the last Emperor of the Julio-Claudian Dynasty.

4. Rome invaded Judea in 67 CE with Vespian Flavius as Commander and his son Titus Flavius as second in Command. After Nero killed himself in 68 CE, Vespian left to take over Rome as Emperor and Titus took over as Commander. Titus successfully laid waste to Jerusalem that 'only the desert was left'. Before Vespian took over there was a brief period of civil wars called the Year of the Four Emperors. Vespian was the fourth successive Emperor in one year.

5. When Vespian died, Titus took over as Emperor in 79 CE then Mt Vesuvius erupted and killed thousands of people in Naples. Titus was remembered for helping the people of Naples. Just 2 years later, Emperor Titus Flavius died. The Jews were saying he was punished by God for destroying the temple. One rumor was he had been poisoned and the other rumor was he had a tumor in his head caused by an insect God send to eat his brain.

6. Titus Flavius's younger brother Domitian took over as Emperor.

It was just a continuous chain of disasters. You cannot help thinking that there is something seriously wrong with Rome at that time!

Was it divine revenge or just random disasters? Our test of significance suggest it was caused by something and it can only be the 'hand of God'.

2. Crucifixion of Jesus Christ

There is an interesting parallel in St Paul's story to Jesus himself. Jesus was sentenced to death by the Jewish Leaders and they all perished with their beloved Jerusalem and Temple. Jerusalem as Jesus had already predicted will be destroyed. It happened in 70 CE, just 37 years from his crucifixion.

We have to ask the question. Was it divine wrath that destroyed Jerusalem in 70 CE as Titus Flavius, commander of the Roman Army claims? Only the desert was left by the Romans where the city of Jerusalem once stood.

We can see the continuous punishment that God had dished out to the Jews and Romans alike after the crucifixion and decapitation of St Paul.

In Matthew 24: 1-2, Mark 13:1-2 and Luke 21: 5-6 Jesus predicted the destruction of the temple

Jesus left the temple and was walking away when his disciples came up to him to call his attention to its buildings. "Do you see all these things?" he asked. "Truly I tell you, not one stone here will be left on another; every one will be thrown down.

3. Pontius Pilate was canonised

Pontius Pilate who washed his hands from the blood of Jesus was saved. He was summoned to Rome to answer charges for a riot of Samaritans in Jerusalem but the Emperor Tiberius died before Pontius Pilate got there, and was replaced by Emperor Galigula. It effectively saved Pilate from a cruel fate. As it happened, Pilate became St Pilate in the years to come! Here's an excerpt from History Today;

In the Gospel of Matthew, Pilate's wife warns her husband not to harm Jesus and for this she achieved sainthood among Orthodox Christians. The Copts and Christians of Ethiopia took the next step and canonised Pilate himself. An Ethiopian collection of hagiographies lists St Pilate's Day as the 25th of the summer month of Sanne, a day shared with his wife Procla and the saints Jude, Peter and Paul:

> *Salutation to Pilate, who washed his hands*
> *To show he himself was innocent of the blood of*
> *Jesus Christ*

Hope in God and God's help

Paul is credited with writing 13 of the 27 books of the new testament, the book of Hebrews is thought to have been written by his followers using his writings. The problems with the Jews and also the Romans had put Paul under house arrest for 2 years in Rome, around 60 CE, yet he continued to preach the gospel. It is fairly obvious why hope was so important to Paul, in his writings.

In 1 Timothy, 4:10 Paul talks about his hope in God;

That is why we labor and strive, because we have put our hope in the living God, who is the Savior of all people, and especially of those who believe.

It is very interesting that these events occurred before the First Jewish-Roman War (66-73 CE) and destruction of the City of Jerusalem and its Second Temple in 70 C.E.

We are given a glimpse of what is going on by the words of Titus Flavius, the Roman Commander. Upon his return to Rome, a victory arch known as the Arch of Titus was built in his honour, which can still be seen in Rome today. It was rumored he refused to accept a wreath of victory saying that he was just effecting 'Divine Wrath' on the Jews!.

This first Jewish-Roman war destroyed the Jews completely. About 1.1 million people were killed by the Roman Army because it was the time of Passover and many Jews had come to Jerusalem to celebrate. After this war in 73 CE, the Jews were reduced from a majority in Judea to scattered minorities, around the region, who were persecuted everywhere for almost 2,000 years.

Just as an aside to this piece of history was the establishment of the modern State of Israel in 1948. It was the Christians who 1. saved the Jews from being exterminated by Hitler and the Nazis 2. resurrected the State of Israel and repatriated all the Jews from around the world to Israel as their new home.

I guess in the final establishment of a home for the Jews, in 1948, after Judea was destroyed by the Romans in 70 CE, a kind of hope and trust in the human family was returned.

It does give the words of Jesus Christ more strength and credibility. Love your enemies.

In Matthew 5:44, Jesus said,

But I say unto you, Love your enemies, bless them that curse you, do good to them that hate you, and pray for them which despitefully use you, and persecute you.

St Paul's writings gives us a glimpse of the meaning of hope, it is the yearning for the Kingdom of Heaven as promised by Jesus Christ.

The accounts of OBEs and NDEs have given us an idea of what death is like and what spirits experience but only 'outside the gate'. No one has gone through the gate and come back to tell about it.

What is behind the gate?

That must be what St Paul means when he said, we should 'wait patiently for what we do not see is our hope'.

CHAPTER 3.

LOVE

Love for ourselves and others

No one can describe love better than the apostle Paul, in Corinthians 13, Paul wrote;

' If I speak in the tongues of men or of angels, but do not have love, I am only a resounding gong or a clanging cymbal. If I have the gift of prophecy and can fathom all mysteries and all knowledge, and if I have a faith that can move mountains, but do not have love, I am nothing. If I give all I possess to the poor and give over my body to hardship that I may boast, but do not have love, I gain nothing.

Love is patient, love is kind. It does not envy, it does not boast, it is not proud. It does not dishonor others, it is not self-seeking, it is not easily angered, it keeps no record of wrongs. Love does not delight in evil but rejoices with the truth. It always protects, always trusts, always hopes, always perseveres.

Love never fails. But where there are prophecies, they will cease; where there are tongues, they will be stilled; where there is knowledge, it will pass away. For we know in part and we prophesy in part, but when completeness comes, what is in part disappears. When I was a child, I talked like a child, I thought like a child, I reasoned like a child. When I became a man, I put the ways of childhood behind me. For now we see only a reflection as in a mirror; then we shall see face to face. Now I know in part; then I shall know fully, even as I am fully known. And now these three remain: faith, hope and love. But the greatest of these is love.'

This is one of the most famous passages in the Bible and in all of Christianity. Its timelessness and pure divine wisdom can only be the revelations of Christ to Paul. It is the yard stick that we measure ourselves against and as always we find that we still need to do more. We need to examine our thoughts and actions, we need to examine our motivations in the light of this revelation about love. Love it seems is the state of holiness, a pure state of being one with Christ. It is interesting to note that in accounts of OBEs and NDEs, they feel love and see beauty in everything in the world of the spirits. Was Paul talking about that world? Where the spirits become one with God?

I suggest that the 'point of no return' in the spirit world, which I refer to as the 'gate' is when the spirit become one with God.

Love for God

Love is very important in Christianity. Not only the love for ourselves and others but we must also love God.

In Matthew 22: 37-40, Jesus said,

Jesus replied: "'Love the Lord your God with all your heart and with all your soul and with all your mind.' This is the first and greatest commandment. And the second is like it: 'Love your neighbor as yourself.' All the Law and the Prophets hang on these two commandments."

Loving God is straight forward, but loving thy neighbour can be a challenge. First of all, who is thy neighbour? The people next door? Your fellow workers, your fellow sports team mates?

In the broader sense, neighbor can mean everybody that is known to you and those you meet. It is not hard to see why, if you apply love as explained by St Paul to everything and everybody you know, there will be such a loving and peaceful world as a result.

References to Love in the Bible

Love is so important in the Christian faith that in both the gospels and St Paul's writings love is emphasized, repeatedly.

Love is a key ingredient of being a Christian, love allows one to have faith, love allows one to have hope, love allows one to feel charitable.

You stay with your wife and children because you love them. You like to do things for them without expecting them to give you anything. When you are in need, you have faith and hope that those you love will come and help you. Similarly, because you love God you also have faith in God.

In fact, love and faith go hand in hand in our meditation of the infinite.

St Paul's description of love is worth repeating. We should make it a mantra for our everyday living to repeat St Paul's passage on love to ourselves everyday, especially the first two paragraphs.

1 Corinthians 13:4-8

Love is patient, love is kind. It does not envy, it does not boast, it is not proud. It does not dishonor others, it is not self-seeking, it is not easily angered, it keeps no record of wrongs. Love does not delight in evil but rejoices with the truth. It always protects, always trusts, always hopes, always perseveres.

Love never fails. But where there are prophecies, they will cease; where there are tongues, they will be stilled; where there is knowledge, it will pass away.

Love as Charity

1 Corinthians 16:14

Let all your things be done with charity.

Charity is big business in the world to day. This kind of charity is the collection of money or raising money to help the poor and disadvantaged in our society.

According to *www.philantrophy.com*, there were a total of 1.2 charities and private organizations in 2009, that work towards alleviating the disadvantaged situations of the poor. These were numbers provided in the United States but there is an interesting development in world charity donations.

Most global charities began with the idea of the teachings of Jesus Christ and his apostles. However, it seems that other religions are also becoming more charitable.

A list of the 10 most charitable nations in the world, in Wikipedia, are 1. United States 2. Myanmar 3. New Zealand 4. Australia 5. Ireland 6. Canada 7. United Kingdom 8. Netherlands 9. Sri Lanka 10. Indonesia. What is surprising is that Myanmar which is a low income country is the second most charitable in the world. Sr Lanka is also another low income country but is the ninth most charitable in the world. These nations have a majority Theravada Buddhists who regularly donate money as a matter of religious giving! The other surprise is Indonesia which is also a low income country but is a majority Moslem country.

It appears that being charitable, as a Christian virtue, is also catching on in other religions.

I have no doubt that most humans are charitable in nature, but we don't get to hear about it.

God is Love

1 John 4:8

Whoever does not love does not know God, because God is love.

The accounts of both Mark and Matthew on Jesus's answer to questions by a Pharisee expert on Jewish law. A Pharisee is a member of an ancient Jewish sect in Judaea, at the time of Jesus distinguished by strict observance of the traditional and written law, and commonly held to have pretensions to superior sanctity.

The answer is about love for God. In this situation both the Pharisees and Sadducees were trying to test Jesus.

Sadducees were also an ancient Jewish sect or party of the time of Christ that denied the resurrection of the dead, the existence of spirits, and the obligation of oral tradition, emphasizing acceptance of the written Law alone.

In Mark 12: 29-31, Jesus is recorded to say;

The most important one, answered Jesus, is this: Hear, O Israel: The Lord our God, the Lord is one. Love the Lord your God with all your heart and with all your soul and with all your mind and with all your strength. The second is this: Love your neighbor as yourself. There is no commandment greater than these.

In Matthew 22: 36-40, Jesus is recorded to say;

Teacher, which is the greatest commandment in the Law?

Jesus replied: 'Love the Lord your God with all your heart and with all your soul and with all your mind.' This is the first and greatest commandment. And the second is like it: Love your neighbor as yourself.

Obviously, the proposals by Jesus Christ were in conflict with the views of the Pharisees and Sadducees who regard themselves as experts on Jewish Law. This conflict became apparent later when the 'Jewish Law' was used against Jesus in his crucifixion.

Love as proposed by St Paul and Jesus Christ were not in the vocabulary of the Jewish High Priests, Pharisees and Sadducees.

This is an important and significant window into the world of the Jews during the time of Jesus. Love, as proposed by St Paul, was completely absent in the Jewish world, which is probably why everyone who were regarded as a 'heretic' or preaching against Jewish Law is immediately killed by a 'mob of angry Jews'.

How can you claim to live by the letter of the Law when you do not love your neighbour?

It does seem that somebody need to preach moderation to the biblical Jews. As Jesus told the mob trying to stone a 'loose woman'.

In John 8:7, Jesus said;

'Let any one of you who is without sin be the first to throw a stone at her.'

John 13: 34-35

A new command I give you: Love one another. As I have loved you, so you must love one another. By this everyone will know that you are my disciples, if you love one another.

Jesus knew that love is absent from the Jewish nation of his day. The punishment was usually very severe for breaking the Jewish Law based on the 10 commandments. Stoning of lawbreakers was a regular event. Imagine a mob stoning a prostitute in the town square in 2020!

Jesus Christ was the voice of moderation and forgiveness. He even stopped a stoning and told the prostitute to go home and 'sin no more'.

What we are seeing is a place full of violence in the name of the law. Archaeologists also found a place full of disease where most children die before adolescence. Tuberculosis, syphilis and leprosy were diseases reported to be very common in Judaea at the time of Jesus.

The picture of a very disadvantaged society begin to emerge, which was also heavily taxed by the Romans.

No wonder the Messiah was so important to the Israelis. They really need someone to deliver them from their problems.

In Hinduism and Buddhism, the avatar is a God which take on human form to help man and teach them in times of great need. We know from the records alone, everything that happened in the past 2,000 years that Jesus Christ cannot possibly be a man. The things he did, the prophecies he foretold and the knowledge he had were much more advanced for any human of his time.

That is why his disciples believe that he was God the Son, and they were willing to die in his name and for the sake of his gospel. So what did Jesus Christ come to teach man as God's avatar?

Well, over the past 2,000 years Christianity has taken over the world. Love is much more valued now than 2,000 years ago. Millions of people give money to help the poor and feed the hungry without expecting anything in return. Most people in the world have values that are 'Christ like' even though they do not go to church.

All of that goodness could not have happened by accident and survival of the fittest. We do believe that God took on human form to teach man what we are experiencing to day, an advanced society, where love and empathy for the less fortunate is a virtue worth having.

Love for your fellow men

It is not an easily achievable virtue to love everyone you know and meet. We all know that, even in our own families we tend to fight and be miserable but those are the people we love the most.

How can we profess that we love everybody when we fail in our own personal relationships?. It does also apply today, it seems love is absent from our world but interestingly enough, every OBE and NDE experience relate an 'experience filled with warmth and love'. The world of the spirits is filled with love and beauty.

Is that why God is portrayed as love?

Left to our own designs, we will probably be still killing each other like they did in ancient times up to the end of World War II. Men do not seem to have any patience or forgiveness for each other.

When Captain James Cook visited the Pacific Island of Tonga in 1773, 1774 and 1777 he recorded a lot of the local customs and traditions. One custom was really shocking in his view.

When he arrived one time for a meeting, a Chief was clearing the way and organizing everybody. When a young man was too slow to move, the Chief hit him , on the head, with a club. The young man fell down, blood coming out of his ears, nose and mouth. His legs kicking and body convulsing and the Chief ordered the other young people to take him away.

When the incident was mentioned by Cook to him later, when it was known the kid had died, he just laughed and dismissed it. It is the local custom that if you do not obey your Chief, you can be killed with a single club smash on the head, as if its the Chief's right. No one will even question the Chief for that decision. Common people can be killed like dogs and no one will care.

Captain James Cook, despite all the negatives, did give Tonga the name 'Friendly Islands' because the locals had put on a feast and entertainment for him and his crew. One visit lasted 3 months!

Clearly in societies where there is no Christ like teachings for people to follow, the rule of the jungle is the norm.

The famous verses of love

Here are some of the most famous verses about love in the Christian Bible. We have already read the most passage by St Paul on love in Corinthians chapter 13.

Let's look at those.

Colossians 3:14

And over all these virtues put on love, which binds them all together in perfect unity

Love can bring us together to work and help each other. In all Christian societies, all over the world, working together in peace and harmony is the most obvious trait. There is tolerance and love for all members of that society.

The strong helps the weak and the learned help the trainees. All the members of society have a common goal in improving and helping one another.

John 15:13

Greater love hath no man than this, that a man lay down his life for his friends.

This verse is obviously a reference to Christ who gave his life for those of his friends, but more importantly he brought the whole world together through his teachings. The crucifixion is not merely to demonstrate Gods power but also to create it. How does God's power work through death?

God's power is not only death but resurrection. A clear statement that life does not end with death, that life continues after death.

The behavior of the Jews is a clear indication of the kind of people they were in Biblical Days. It is no surprise they have been persecuted for more than 2,000 years. Only the love of Christ saved the Jewish nation and brought the Jews home after being kicked out by Islam for more than a 1,000 years.

Do you think it is an accident that the State of Israel was resurrected?

It is predicted in the Bible that Israel will be destroyed because its people have lost their way. But God will bring them back, through Jesus Christ.

The power of the word.

John 3:16

For God so loved the world, that he gave his only begotten Son, that whosoever believeth in him should not perish, but have everlasting life.

This is one of the most powerful verses in the Bible. It clearly lays out the reason and the why for Christians. God gave his son to earth to show them the way. If they believe in his teachings, they will have eternal life through him. In the OBE and NDE experiences, it is clear there is a place that the souls go after the body dies. Some have also met Jesus Christ and were told to return and fulfil their purposes in life.

1 John 4:19

We love him, because he first loved us.

God loves man unconditionally. This is the meaning of grace. God's unmerited love for man. The declaration that we love God is a acknowledgement of God's grace.

1 John 4:7

Beloved, let us love one another: for love is of God; and every one that loveth is born of God, and knoweth God.

It is true that essence of the teachings of Christ is about love. As we have read already, love is a product of faith and through faith we learn to love one another.

This is an important Christian phenomena, faith in Christ gives the believer love like Christ. We always fall short as written in Pauls epistle to the Corinthians chapter 13 but we know what to do. We do what Christ teaches us in the Lord's prayer.

We forgive those that trespass against us. Forgiveness is a product of love, just as love is a product of faith. We forgive everyday, just like God gives us our bread, everyday.

We all know it is hard but we should try.

John 14:15

If ye love me, keep my commandments.

Obedience is another product of love. When we love we forgive others and obey God's commandments.

1 John 4: 18

There is no fear in love; but perfect love casteth out fear: because fear hath torment. He that feareth is not made perfect in love.

Love as already pointed out is a product of faith. Faith is an instrument of Christ. Because of our faith in Christ we can love like Christ. We can forgive those that trespass against us, not once, but everyday.

We learn to love those who hate and persecute us because it is what Christ commanded and because it is the right thing to do.

No where this is more apparent, then in global charity. Christians reach out to all people in all walks of life who need help. Who need clothes. Who need a roof above their heads and food on the table.

We shall discuss this Christian attribute more in the next chapter.

CHAPTER 4

CHARITY

Charity is often interchangeable with love, but it should be explained as a separate act. In Luke 21:1-4, the apostle points to a different aspect of charity.

As Jesus looked up, he saw the rich putting their gifts into the temple treasury. He also saw a poor widow put in two very small copper coins. "Truly I tell you," he said, "this poor widow has put in more than all the others. All these people gave their gifts out of their wealth; but she out of her poverty put in all she had to live on.

In 2 Corinthians 9:6-8

Remember this: Whoever sows sparingly will also reap sparingly, and whoever sows generously will also reap generously. Each of you should give what you have decided in your heart to give, not reluctantly or under compulsion, for God loves a cheerful giver.

Charity, in Christian thought, is the highest form of love, signifying the reciprocal love between God and man that is made manifest in unselfish love of one's fellow men. Paul's classical description of charity is found in I Corinthian 13.

But charity as understood by most people is the art of giving without expectations of a return. This kind of giving is with the understanding that one's money will benefit the less fortunate.

Many people give to charity because it is right but also there is good karma in it. As we have seen in our paragraph about charities in the world, the countries of Myanmar and Sri Lanka are poor by world standards, yet they are among the top 10 most charitable nations. Why? It turns out that both countries have a majority of Theravada Buddhism which encourage giving to charity as a regular religious offering.

Indonesia is a Moslem country but features highly in charity donations. Islam also encourages giving to charity, in fact the most charitable people in many countries are Moslems.

In Proverbs 19:17

"Whoever is kind to the poor lends to the Lord, and he will reward them for what they have done."

Many people like to give because it makes them feel good. Loving the poor also implies love for the Lord who has commanded that we do to those less fortunate people what we would do for him.

Again, it is such a difficult path to follow and very similar to 'turning the other cheek'.

We have spoken before why people leave and become hermits probably because they can find themselves closer to God in isolation.

Charity begins at home

The Catechism of the Catholic Church defines "charity" as "the theological virtue by which we love God above all things for His own sake, and our neighbor as ourselves for the love of God".

Be generous to your family before helping others. For example, don't spend hours and hours on volunteer work and neglect the children, forgetting that charity begins at home.

In New Zealand, most of the violence reported to the Police every 4 minutes are between family members. The statistics also suggest that most homicides in New Zealand are by people known to the victims with family members killing each other high on the list!

There is a very urgent call for families to be saved from violence, but how can we do it? How can we save family members from tearing each other apart. They live together everyday and will always have some disagreements but how can we teach them not to kill each other?

This is a situation similar to the time of Jesus Christ, there is a great need for a savior to save New Zealand families from violence. A huge compounding effect is the problem with mental health which has snowballed in recent years. A former Minister of Health, Dr Jonathan Coleman, was quoted in the New Zealand media that 800,000 Kiwis have been through the Mental Health Department of the Ministry of Health. Experts were also quoted that mental health numbers could be as high as 2 million in 10 years time.

That is almost 50% of the country experiencing mental health problems! The problem of homelessness has somehow been alleviated during the covid19 period when all homeless people were housed in the empty hotels to keep any infections from being spread around. However, the long term issues remain.

How can Christ and his teachings help mental health issues and homeless people?

These are big issues for charity organizations worldwide. One of the first aid approaches is to help the kids while they are young to avoid later problems in life.

Our small Tongan community at Northcote, Auckland was affected by youth issues and law breaking problems. More than 10 youths were jailed for various minor offences. It was a big number for the less than 50 or so Tongan families in the area. The elders got together over a kava bowl and discussed the issues. We established a Trust called the Project Revival Charity Trust (Inc) to help our youth revive their future and good standing in the community. One of our very first programmes was promoting reading to our kids. It is known that reading can improve decision making, in prison inmates but could also apply to the general population.

Our Trust has been operating for 7 years helping our families and we hope to expand it and establish a school or university for the kids in the near future. I am the current Chief Executive.

Purpose of charity

A charity must have one or more of the purposes which have been defined in law. These include things like relieving poverty, education, religion, protecting the environment, animal welfare, human rights and community development.

These charities are supported by government and can sought donations from the public, however there are other less known charities which are equally effective.

Biblical charity is about the love of Christ. He fed 5,000 people, he healed the sick and the blind, he showed a prostitute the right way, he advised the rich and poor on how to live a good clean life. He showed the world that it is possible to live after death.

All these Christ like attributes are being carried out by charities throughout the world giving housing and feeding the poor, providing medicine for the sick, teaching people the right way to live and budget their money and so on.

What is the meaning of charity?

Charity is defined as generous actions or donations to aid the poor, ill, or helpless or giving to a person or persons in need.

Charity is love. Christians believe that God's love and generosity towards humanity moves and inspires us to love and be generous in response. Jesus taught that to love God and to love your neighbour are the greatest commandments. Charity is not an optional extra, but an essential component of faith.

What about your family?

We have already discussed that one's charitable actions should start at home and if this is so it would solve the problems of family violence. Family members killing each other.

Evangelical Christianity

There are a large number of charities in the name of Jesus Christ. They are the sign of a sincere and grateful faith. They include actions for the 'great commission', evangelism, service in the church and family.

The Chronicle of Philanthropy put the number of charities and foundations in the world at 1.2 million, who spent $US 410.2 billion annually to help those in need. It has been quoted that 85 cents in every dollar goes to people in need.

This is a huge number, its more than twice the GDP of New Zealand which was quoted as $205 billion in 2019!

The World Bank estimates that 40 million to 60 million people will fall into extreme poverty (under $1.90/day) in 2020, compared to 2019, as a result of COVID-19, depending on assumptions on the magnitude of the economic shock. This maybe a bit more than normal but it does show the huge global problem of poverty which also bring sickness, homelessness, high mortality rates and so on with it.

The need for Christians to do more is greater than ever, reaching out with the loving and healing hands of Christ and show the poor and destitute the meaning of charity.

One of the problems as I see it is that in many cases the extreme poor in the world are of other religious denominations and they do not understand the charity of Christ. They were raised in a non-Christian society where their values are a little different. In order for them to understand the charity of Christ, they must convert and become Christians.

I now understand why Billy Graham tried so hard to convert the whole world to Christ. In the end, before he died he admitted defeat. He says that he was unable to convert the world's population to Christianity.

If I had something to say to Billy Graham, I would tell him that he did not fail. He did save many more lives than most people in many life times. But like St Paul's conversion by Christ, I believe that Christ is firmly holding the cause in a straight line.

It did occur to me there is another dimension to the teachings of Christ as shown by OBE and NDE individuals. It seems that they experienced the love of Christ after death. Almost all their accounts tell of an existence more real than the one they left behind, full of love and beauty and they see and feel God and Christ in everything. I suppose Billy Graham has already found it out himself.

The meaning is that, even if you did not find Christ in this life, you will certainly meet him in the next one.

Countries that help strangers

The five countries ranked highest for helping a stranger were Liberia, Sierra Leone, the U.S., Kenya and Zambia. The five countries reporting the highest percentage of respondents saying they had donated money were Myanmar, the United Kingdom, Malta, Thailand and the Netherlands.

In this survey, quoted by google, I again reiterate the fact that being charitable is not unique to western Christians but are also found in other cultures. It does suggest that many are practising the 5 pillars of Christ.

A note on charities

Charity is big business and it is always a good idea to check how they are doing. In many countries charities must meet standards, including adequate board oversight and strong conflict-of-interest policies, as well as the requirement that they spend at least 65 percent of their total expenses on their charitable programs and no more than 35 percent of their salaries.

According to google, the Chief Executive Officers of 78 charities were paid between $500,000 and $1 million. For example, the CEO of the Boys and Girls Club of America earned the highest pay in the group of $1.85 million, according to the survey.

One explanation that is always given is that because charity is big business, the CEO salaries must be on a bar with similar organizations and businesses of the same size.

I would say that preferably, they should work for free but there is always a problem with their family and personal needs that require monetary supply. For example, I am the CEO of our Project Revival Charity

Trust (Inc) and I don't get paid for what I do for the Trust. It is still a small group but someday it will grow much bigger and staff may need to be hired and paid.

Charity according to St Peter

St Paul is the most prolific writer of all the apostles and we are getting familiar with Paul's ideas. But here is a verse from St Peter.

1 Peter 4:8

And above all things have fervent charity among yourselves: for charity shall cover the multitude of sins.

St Peter is reminding everyone of the call from the Lord that we must love one another. In that process of love we will overcome sin. Love is a product of faith, the same as obedience. If we have faith then love and obedience are its products. We will love and obey the Lord when we have faith in him.

We will also love and obey one another when we have faith in the Lord and ourselves the precursors of a charitable heart.

CHAPTER 5

SPIRITUAL SALVATION

Christ the redeemer

Jesus Christ's main objective is spiritual salvation which was a new approach to the Jewish law. He did say that I have come to complete the law, or fulfill it.

In Matthew 5: 16-17, Jesus said

In the same way, let your light shine before men, that they may see your good deeds and glorify your Father in heaven. Do not think that I have come to abolish the Law or the Prophets. I have not come to abolish them, but to fulfill them.

  The Jews believe that God made a covenant with them, probably the same one housed in the ark of the covenant, and God rewards good deeds and punish evil. They do not believe in spiritual salvation as proposed by Christ because the messiah has not come yet. It is interesting to note that Jews believe salvation will come when they are saved from their exiles especially the current one…meaning the one before 1948. Jesus Christ and his followers have given the Jews a homeland thus saving them according to the scriptures.

Salvation in Christianity, or deliverance or redemption, is the *"saving of human beings from death and separation from God"* by Christ's death and resurrection.

The death of Christ and his resurrection is the key to salvation, as explained by OBE and NDE experiences. When humans die they also experience another life. A life so real that many propose 'we are spirits having a human experience'. Salvation is connection with that next life.

I did mention in the introduction the comment by Pope Francis that souls who do not return to God are simply lost. This has put great significance on the parable of the lost sheep. Christ saved us from being lost.

Why do we need to be saved?

In Hinduism, it is believed that desires and delusions are keeping us away from our calling. It keeps us trapped in the never ending cycle of death and rebirth into a very unsatisfactory existence which we should escape from, reincarnation. The only way to escape is to do good deeds and accumulate good karma to attain moksha or the state of being saved and returning to the Cosmic Spirit or God. A similar state in Buddhism is called nirvana.

It does fit in with what Jesus Christ refer to as being 'forgiven of our sins' so that we may return to God. That is spiritual salvation according to Christ. Instead of spending our time doing good deeds by ourselves, we believe in Christ and follow his teachings to achieve forgiveness of our sins. It is sin that is preventing us from being saved. When we accept Christ as our savior, we become one with him. Our sins are cleansed and we achieve the state of being holy, the Christian nirvana.

A holy person does not sin and is Godlike being one with Christ, God the Son.

As explained in our chapter on the Trinity, being one with God can elevate us into an existence with no beginning or end, where time does not exist.

In Theology

In religion and theology, salvation is the saving of the soul from sin and its consequences. It may also be called deliverance or redemption from sin and its effects.

In Ephesians 2:8, St Paul proposes

'For it is by grace that you have been saved because of your faith - and it is not from you but by the love of God'.

I wrote the book 'God is Energy. Do You Believe' 3 on this very idea by St Paul. Grace is God's unmerited love for man which includes the coming of Christ, his death and resurrection and spiritual salvation.

Some excerpts from google - gift of salvation

The gift of salvation is the gift of sanctification, by word and Spirit. The light that God graciously gives is the revelation of Himself.

a person or thing that is the means of preserving from harm. Christianity deliverance by redemption from the power of sin and from the penalties ensuing from it. Christian Science the realization that Life, Truth, and Love are supreme and that they can destroy such illusions as sin and death.

Faith in Jesus Christ

By having faith in Jesus, Christians believe they receive God's grace . This means they believe God has blessed them, which in turn gives them the strength to live a good Christian life.
Ultimately, salvation from sin was the purpose of Jesus' life, death and resurrection.

PART V

THE TRUTH ABOUT THE BIBLE AND JESUS CHRIST

Chapter 1.

Titus Flavius

There is a lot of publications and scholars who are saying that the story of Jesus Christ was invented by the Romans. In particular, Titus Flavius conquerer of Jerusalem in the year 70 CE (Christian Era). Titus Flavius was the son of Vespian Flavius who succeeded Emperor Nero in 67 CE.

Vespian was actually the Commander of the Roman Army send to destroy Jerusalem in 66 CE, after the Jewish revolt and take over of the city, but during the campaign Emperor Nero died and Vespian returned to Rome and took over as Emperor. Titus was left to finish the job of sacking Jerusalem and destroying it. Titus did a very good job laying waste to Jerusalem and the surrounding countryside.

Titus succeeded Vespian in 79 CE but himself died in 81 CE and his younger brother Domitian took over.

There was a rumor that Domitian had actually poisoned his older brother in order to take over as emperor. His ambitions was well known but Titus ignored them and according to some historians, paid the ultimate price. He is recorded as saying, 'I have made but one mistake in my life' but not really elaborating on what it was; on his death bed.

The Vespian Flavius dynasty lasted until about 95 CE with the death of Emperor Domitian in 96 CE when he was assassinated by court officials because of his ruthless and harsh treatment of the Senate. It was during the rule of the Flavius Dynasty (67-96 CE), the critics say, the plot of inventing Christ was hatched.

The arguments are very complicated and needs careful analysis but suffice it to say that the proposal was, **the Romans thought it would be easier to control their subjects as believers**. So the Romans invented Jesus Christ and created the Christian Kingdom based in Rome with the Pope at its head.

The success of the Christians is actually attributed to the Romans when Christianity was made the official religion of Rome during the reign of Emperor

Constantine. Constantine himself is said to have accepted Christianity and converted in 312 CE.

It is a bit suspect that it took 200 years before the Roman Empire became Christian. If they had invented Jesus Christ with the aim of converting the world to be Roman subjects it took a rather long time to happen.

Many of the historical records suggest that Christianity became the official religion of Rome from the time of Emperor Constantine in 312 CE.

It is rather unusual for anyone to propose that the Flavius invented Jesus Christ and Christianity because the Roman Empire did not become Christian until 216 years later.

Historical evidence supporting the existence of Jesus Christ

There are also a lot of historical evidence that Jesus Christ did exist. Here are the historical evidence.

1. The Writings

(i) St Paul's epistles from 50-60 CE are the earliest texts mentioning Jesus and the doctrines of Christianity, explaining how followers should practice and live the faith. We should note that St Paul's letters were written a 1-2 decades before Vespian Flavius became Emperor and the supposed conspiracy to invent Christ occurred.

(ii) The first non-Christian to talk about Jesus was the Jewish historian Flavius Josephus around 47-100 CE. He referred to Christ in his history of Judaism, 'Jewish Antiquities' written around 93 CE.

First he referred to Jesus as the brother of James and secondly in a passage from Antiquities 18: 3:3;

> *"There was about this time Jesus, a wise man, if it be lawful to call him a man, for he was a doer of wonderful works —a teacher of such men as receive the truth with pleasure. He drew over to him both many of the Jews, and many of the Gentiles. He was Christ; and when Pilate, at the*

suggestion of the principal men amongst us, had condemned him to the cross, those that loved him at the first did not forsake him, for he appeared to them alive again the third day, as the divine prophets had foretold these and ten thousand other wonderful things concerning him; and the tribe of Christians, so named from him, are not extinct at this day."

(iii) The Roman historians Pliny and Tacitus also wrote about Jesus 20 years after the book by Josephus.

The "Annals" by Tacitus from 115 CE mentioned the Roman prefect **Pontius Pilate** *executing Jesus, alluding to crucifixion, and placed that event within the time frame that agrees with Christian gospels. As you can also see in this excerpt, Tacitus was not a big fan of the Christians:*

> *"Nero fastened the guilt and inflicted the most exquisite tortures on a class hated for their abominations, called "Chrestians" by the populace," wrote Tacitus." Christus, from whom the name had its origin, suffered the extreme penalty during the reign of Tiberius at the hands of*

one of our procurators, Pontius Pilate, and a most mischievous superstition, thus checked for the moment, again broke out not only in Judaea, the first source of the evil, but even in Rome, where all things hideous and shameful from every part of the world find their center and become popular. Accordingly, an arrest was first made of all who pleaded guilty; then, upon their information, an immense multitude was convicted, not so much of the crime of firing the city, as of hatred against mankind."

Pliny the Younger, governor of Asia Minor, wrote letters to Emperor Trajan around 112 CE describing Christians worshiping Jesus as a God.

"They (Christians) were in the habit of meeting on a certain fixed day before it was light, when they sang in alternate verses a hymn to Christ, as to a god, and bound themselves by a solemn oath, not to any wicked deeds, but never to commit any fraud, theft or adultery, never to falsify their word, nor deny a trust when they should be called upon to deliver it up; after which it was their custom to separate, and then reassemble to partake of food, but of an ordinary and innocent kind ,"

Pliny the Elder (Gaius Plinius Secundus) wrote in Epistles 10.96. Pliny was a Roman writer who died trying to rescue a friend during the eruption of Mt Vesuvius in 79 CE.

The eruption of Mt Vesuvius was one of the string of problems faced by the Flavius Dynasty.

2. The Eye Witnesses

The earliest Christian writings on Jesus come from the epistles of Paul. The first of these date to no later than within 25 years of Jesus's death (AD 50-60). On the other hand, biographical accounts of Jesus in the New Testament date from around 40 years after Jesus's death. Still, these time spans mean that accounts of Jesus's life were written down by people who would have been alive to know him or the people who knew him personally.

The accounts of the witnesses also correspond quite well to what other sources of information tell us about the life in the Palestine of the first century. For example, having large crowds coming to a healer like Jesus is confirmed through archaeology, which tells us that residents of the area had to contend with diseases like leprosy and tuberculosis. A study of burials in Roman Palestine by archaeologist **Byron McCane** *revealed that between two-thirds and three-quarters of the graves they looked at had remains of children and adolescents. McCane underscored the prevalence of childhood mortality at the time,* **explaining** *that "during Jesus' time, mortality due to disease was high.*

The eye witnesses also include a large number of followers who became Christians in the first century. It is irrefutable and very unlikely that such a large number of people would be wrong or can be tricked!

PART VI

REINCARNATION

Chapter 1.

What the Bible say about karma and reincarnation?

The first mention of any generational connections in the Bible is in the 10 commandments itself. A karma like effect of disobedience to God's commandments. The Israelites were banned from creating an image to replace God and worshiping it, or worshiping any other God, punishment will be delivered to those who disobey. They and their children and grandchildren will be punished, but love for 'a thousand generations', for those who trust and worship him.

It does suggest that karma is very well and alive in the Christian faith and tradition according to the 10 commandments. The Christian equivalent of karma would be sin itself. The greatest enemy of Christianity is sin because sin is a personal decision to disobey God's commandment, to disobey the biblical truth that Christians are supposed to uphold. Very often

Satan, the Evil One, is blamed for causing man to sin or disobey God. The punishment of sin is eternal damnation, a disconnection from God and being lost for eternity.

The death and resurrection of Jesus Christ is a triumph over sin and its consequence of death and eternal damnation. Man can be saved from eternal damnation and sin through faith and trust in Jesus Christ as his saviour. There is a huge difference here between Christianity and Hinduism and Buddhism. Christians expect to be saved through faith in Jesus Christ and his teachings, whereas in Hinduism and Buddhism, one is saved by one's own good deeds thus accumulating good karma. Christianity is very similar in dogma to Islam, in that faith and trust in God is the ultimate salvation.

> Main points…
>
> In Hinduism and Buddhism, man saves himself by seeking enlightenment and doing good to escape the cycle of death and rebirth. In Christianity and Islam, man is saved by faith in God who bestow his grace upon them.

In Exodus 20: 3-6, God's commandment is very clear;

You shall have no other gods before me.

'You shall not make for yourself an image in the form of anything in heaven above or on the earth beneath or in the waters below. You shall not bow down to them or worship them; for I, the LORD your God, am a jealous God, punishing the children for the sin of the parents to the third and fourth generation of those who hate me, but showing love to a thousand generations of those who love me and keep my commandments.'

This is what Jesus Christ say about sin.

In Luke 19:10 he says;

'For the son of man came to save the lost'

The biggest problem with man is his relationship with God. He is the 'lost sheep' which Jesus refers to in his parables. God will reach out to save the one lost sheep. It is very clear from the Bible and Christ's teachings that man need God as his saviour. Man's faith will be his salvation through God's grace. That is how man can escape and return to God.

In most of the OBEs and NDEs on record, the experience is such a wonderful and loving existence in a world full of love and beauty that they did not want to come back. They believe and feel that the world they had entered is the real world and earth is just an 'unsatisfactory existence' as they say in Hinduism.

That is probably where the Hinduism and Buddhism idea of reincarnation come from. The experience of OBE and NDE individuals.

There are also records of Hindu and Buddhists who are able to achieve 'a cross over' through meditation techniques.

It must be pointed out that while Hinduism have many Gods, Buddhism only believe in man and his actions to achieve nirvana, the equivalent of the Hindu moksha. In other words, Buddhism do not believe in Gods.

In 1 John 3:6 Jesus said; the King James Version and New American Standard Bible puts it clearly in slightly different wordings;

1 John 3:6, KJV: *"Whosoever abideth in him sinneth not: whosoever sinneth hath not seen him, neither known him."*

1 John 3:6, NASB: *"No one who abides in Him sins; no one who sins has seen Him or knows Him."*

The apostle John is referring to those who are holy, the equivalent of moksha (Hinduism) and nirvana (Buddhism), because they do not commit any sin. Sinners do not know Jesus Christ or have achieved the state of being holy in that sense.

It should be said that sinning is a direct result of living in human society where the devil has many tools of temptation. One way of reducing the likelihood of sin is removing oneself from society as in the case of monks in the past. When a devotee of Jesus Christ moves away from society and lives a simple life as a monk or similar group, dedication to Christ and the gospel is possible. Holiness is achievable in that state of solitude, denouncing the worldly goods and pleasures in favor of realization of the gift of Christ and eternity.

It is the same idea practiced in the Catholic Church for centuries. The priests and nuns dedicate themselves to Christ and renounce the world and its temptations, including their own families. Thus devotion to Christ, as a priest or nun, is total and absolute.

The Hindu and Buddhist idea of nirvana or moksha is escaping from the 'unsatisfactory existence on earth' and returning to the Cosmic Spirit known as Brahman. As explained in our example of water in the trinity definition, it is like a drop of water returning to the ocean.

Many of the NDEs and OBEs description include a state of 'super consciousness' after death, where individuals are 'one with everything' knowing everything. This is what Christians refer to as the 'God state' where God is omnipotent and omniscient. **What is the most astounding is the scientific evidence collected also prove the existence of the soul as mentioned in the previous chapters. Although the body is lifeless with no brain activity or heart beat, the person involved awakes and can recall the OBE or NDE as if the soul was a separate entity from the body during death.**

Chapter 2.

Reincarnation according to Hinduism and Buddhism

Hinduism is probably the oldest religion on earth, although many writers also give Judaism the same age as Hinduism. However, if one were to argue that Jesus Christ is God the Son as explained in the Trinity Chapter, then one can say that Christianity is the oldest religion.

Just as the book of John suggest in John 1: 1-5;

In the beginning was the Word, and the Word was with God, and the Word was God. He was with God in the beginning. Through him all things were made; without him nothing was made that has been made. In him was life, and that life was the light of all mankind. The light shines in the darkness, and the darkness has not overcome it.

It is clearly a reference to Jesus Christ, that he existed from the beginning and therefore all who believe in him also believe he was there in the beginning.

Hinduism is explained by some texts as 'a way of life' or culture, even though it is regarded as a religion, in general.

> Reincarnation, a major tenet of Hinduism, is when the soul, which is seen as eternal and part of a spiritual realm, returns to the physical realm in a new body. A soul will complete this cycle many times, learning new things each time and working through its karma. This cycle of reincarnation is called samsara

The basic philosophy of Hinduism is the reincarnation or doctrine of samsara which is the continuous cycle of life, death and rebirth. Reincarnation is affected by karma or the universal law of cause and effect. If one owes a karmic debt, then one is trapped in the continuous reincarnation cycle until one achieves moksha or release from continual rebirth when one realizes that the atman is one with the Brahman.

In that sense, the atman or soul is believed to be the true self. One's existence on earth is to strive for moksha or liberation of the atman from the cycle of rebirth impelled by the law of karma. Like Buddhism,

Hinduism view the endless cycle of reincarnation as a painful and unsatisfactory existence.

It is slightly different in Buddhism where it is believed that suffering is inherent in life and that one can be liberated from it by cultivating wisdom, virtue, and concentration.

Buddhism faith include the four noble truths, 1. existence is suffering (dukhka) 2. suffering has a cause, namely craving and attachment (trishna) 3. there is a cessation of suffering, which is nirvana 4. and there is a path to the cessation of suffering, the middle way, it avoids both indulgence and severe asceticism.

Buddhists believe that rebirth is driven by desire and like the Hindus samsara driven reincarnation which is thought to be painful and unsatisfactory. One's own actions will create a new existence in the after life driving the rebirth. The only escape from this painful existence and unsatisfactory rebirth is the extinguishing of desire.

In Hinduism, very little is attributed to God although there are many Gods. Man is the main creator seeking to end samsara by achieving moksa through overcoming ignorance and desire. Enlightenment through practice of personal moral and seeking wisdom. But desire itself is a paradox because it also includes desire for moksha.

In Buddhism there are no Gods but Buddha and the ultimate aim is the achievement of enlightenment by practicing moral and meditation, relaxing their mind with clear understanding of the law of impermanence, which destroys all attachments, craving, aversion and delusion.

In both religions meat, and certain vegetables, are not consumed, as a general rule, although certain sects will eat meat that is 'offered'.

Hindu population

India has the most Hindus, about 966 million or 80% of the population. Nepal has the largest percentage of Hindu population in the world followed by India and Mauritius. An estimated 60 to 70 million Hindus live outside India.

Buddhist population

Countries with Buddhists majorities include Cambodia (97.9%), Thailand (94.5%), Myanmar (87.9%), Bhutan (74.7%), Sri Lanka (70.2%), Japan (69.8%). China is the country with the largest population of Buddhists, approximately 244 million or 18.2% of its total population.

Chapter 3.

Scientific evidence of the existence of the soul

Although there are many writings on the existence of the soul by various writers as early as Plato and Descartes, no one can give scientific evidence of its existence. Most of the writings has to do with philosophical proposals and logical deductions.

The latest scientific studies have come from 'out of body experience'(OBE) or 'near death experiences' (NDE) recorded by Scientists or the concerned themselves.

A lot of data have been collected by people like Dr Peter Fenwick, for example, among personal stories on You Tube. These stories tell of a really amazing experience by people who were having physical trauma, normally in hospital, which causes their consciousness to leave the body (OBE) and watch it from outside. Many reports watching Doctors trying to revive them and suddenly they are back in the body.

NDEs are also very similar. Patients talk of leaving their body and moving towards a light which is so bright and encompassing usually by people involved in accidents and events where they were considered dead. The first thing they notice is love, they feel incredible love and awareness as if they become part of everything. They meet dead relatives or spirit beings and see flowers of amazing colours and fragrance. Sometimes they talk to 'the light' or dead relatives who tell them to go back because its not their time yet.

One famous NDE is the story of Randy Kay, of Randy Kay Ministries, who was an agnostic, despising religion in general, but since his NDE he is a changed man. Like Saul who became Paul, he is now a crusader for Christ.

What is most amazing from the stories and data collected especially the interview with Dr Peter Fenwick is that 'consciousness exist even when the brain was considered dead!'. Every account on You Tube, of individuals who has had a OBE or NDE, is saying that they had awareness and consciousness when the body and brain are not functioning. It is evidence of the existence of the soul or the spirit being inside every human. The soul can exist out of the body. The soul is described as 'existence of an awareness or consciousness' outside the body which the patient is able to recall when they are revived and come back to life! Obviously the soul is back in the body.

There is also some information on why humans need to learn more about the process of dying and the ease of transition into the universe.

For example, if one is 'attached to worldly goods' then the process of dying may be more distressing as opposed to leaving and joining the light which is full of love and all knowing awareness.

Restarting the heart with a defibrillator

Defibrillation is restarting the heart when it stops. The patient may be experiencing an OBE and as soon as the heart starts again, he or she revives.

One interesting piece of information about the heart is the 'pacemaker' which produces an electric current that causes the heart to contract. This pacemaker is what the defibrillator restarts and causes the heart to beat again sending oxygen into the body through the blood and reviving the patient.

The Pacemaker

Here's what I found on google about the heart's pacemaker. It is called the sinoatrial (SA) node or sinus node. It's a small mass of specialized cells in the top of the right atrium (upper chamber of the heart). It produces the electrical impulses that cause your heart to beat.

When your heart is being restarted using a defibrillator, the electrical current actually causes the SA to start producing impulses again thus causing that phenomena we know as 'reviving the dead'. It could be as easy as reviving the SA!

When we restart the heart, the patient wakes up again and tell a story of what occurs when the body was dead!

If the reviving of the body is simply the restarting of the SA then where is the connection with the soul? It is obvious that there is separation between the body and the soul.

The body sometimes can be revived but it is still dysfunctional as in cases of patients in a coma. A coma can be induced by lack of sugar in the blood in diabetics, brain injury, alcohol poisoning, infection.

The body is asleep and lack consciousness. Obviously when the body is damaged, the soul cannot function or leaves the body!

This may be the subject of our next book. Where does the soul go when you are in a coma!

References

1. Statistics quoted in this book were taken from Wikipedia and Google.
2. Factual historical content were taken from Wikipedia and Google.
3. Many of the author's opinions expressed in this book are supported with others from Google searches and Wikipedia references.
4. Some definitions were obtained from Oxford Definitions.

FURTHER READING

These books, by the same author, can also be found in amazon.com

1. God is Energy. Do You Believe 1
2. God is Energy. Do you Believe 2
3. God is Energy. Do You Believe 3
4. God is Energy. Do You Believe 4
5. God is Energy. Do you Believe 5
6. The Antichrist

ABOUT THE AUTHOR

Semisi Pule also known as Semisi Pule Pone, uses Semisi Pone for short, has been writing about Christianity for 10 years now. He believes that in order for man to understand God and his world he needs to dig deeper into the meaning of it all.

You will notice that the author draws on Hinduism, Buddhism, Islam and even OBE and NDE experiences, in addition to Science to piece together a very comprehensive book on God and life on earth using his own experiences. This book will hopefully help many people understand their spirituality and where they want to be in terms of life after death. But more importantly, where they want to be in this life in the here and now.

The author also writes in other genre with more than 200 books and ebooks in amazon.com.

www.ingramcontent.com/pod-product-compliance
Lightning Source LLC
Chambersburg PA
CBHW072042160426
43197CB00014B/2596